Be In The
Driver's Seat!

GW01081424

J. P. Vaswani

Published by:
GITA PUBLISHING HOUSE
Sadhu Vaswani Mission,
10, Sadhu Vaswani Path, Pune - 411 001, (India).
gph@sadhuvaswani.org

FOR PRIVATE CIRCULATION ONLY

BE IN THE DRIVER'S SEAT!
©2013, J. P. Vaswani
ISBN: 978-93-80743-79-0
1st Edition - 3000 copies - August, 2013
2nd Edition - 3000 copies - September, 2013

DADA VASWANI'S BOOKS
Visit us online to purchase books on self-improvement, spiritual
advancement, meditation and philosophy.
Plus audio cassettes, CDs, DVDs, monthly journals and books in Hindi.
www.dadavaswanisbooks.org

Printed by:
MEHTA OFFSET PVT. LTD.
Mehta House,
A-16, Naraina Industrial Area II,
New Delhi - 110 028. (India).
info@mehtaoffset.com

Be In The
Driver's Seat!

J. P. Vaswani

Gita Publishing House,
PUNE, (India).
www.dadavaswanisbooks.org

Books and Booklets by J.P. Vaswani

7 Commandments of the Bhagavad Gita

10 Commandments of a Successful Marriage

100 Stories You Will Never Forget

108 Pearls of Practical Wisdom

108 Simple Prayers of a Simple Man

108 Thoughts on Success

114 Thoughts on Love

A Little Book of Life

A Little Book of Wisdom

A Simple and Easy Way To God

A Treasure of Quotes

Around The Camp Fire

Be An Achiever

Begin the Day with God

Bhagavad Gita in a Nutshell

Burn Anger Before Anger Burns You

Comrades of God – Lives of Saints from East & West

Daily Appointment with God

Daily Inspiration (A Thought For Every Day Of The Year)

Daily Inspiration

Destination Happiness

Dewdrops of Love

Does God Have Favorites

Finding Peace of Mind

Formula for Prosperity

Friends Forever

Gateways to Heaven

God In Quest of Man

Good Parenting

How to Overcome Depression

I am a Sindhi

I Luv U, God!

India Awake!

Joy Peace Pills

Kill Fear Before Fear Kills You

Ladder of Abhyasa

Lessons Life Has Taught Me

Life after Death

Life and Teachings of Sadhu Vaswani

Life and Teachings of the Sikh Gurus

Living in the Now

Management Moment by Moment

Mantras For Peace Of Mind

Mantras for the Modern Man

Many Paths: One Goal

Many Scriptures: One Wisdom

Nearer, My God, To Thee!

New Education Can Make the World New

Peace or Perish: There Is No Other Choice

Positive Power of Thanksgiving

Questions Answered

Saints For You and Me

Saints With A Difference

Say No to Negatives

Secrets of Health And Happiness

Shake Hands With Life

Short Sketches of Saints Known & Unknown

Sketches of Saints Know & Unknown

Spirituality in Daily Life

Stop Complaining: Start Thanking!

Swallow Irritation Before Irritation Swallows You

Teachers are Sculptors

The Goal Of Life and How To Attain It

The Highway To Happiness

The Little Book of Freedom from Stress

The Little Book of Prayer

The Little Book of Service

The Little Book of Success

The Little Book of Yoga

The Magic of Forgiveness

The Miracle of Forgiving

The New Age Diet: Vegetarianism for You and Me

The Perfect Relationship: Guru and Disciple

The Terror Within

The Way of Abhyasa (How To Meditate)

Thus Have I Been Taught

Tips For Teenagers

What You Would Like To Know About Karma?

What You Would Like To Know About Hinduism?

What To Do When Difficulties Strike?

Why Do Good People Suffer?

Women: Where Would The World Be Without You?

Why Be Sad?

You Are Not Alone: God Is With You!

You Can Change Your Life: Live— Don't Just Exist

Life is a kaleidoscope of events; sometimes the colors are bright and sometimes they are dim and dull. It is a journey filled with myriad experiences that can spell darkness or sunshine. The road of life twists and turns and no two pathways are ever the same. Some times we may stumble upon hardships, heartaches, hindrances and at other times we may encounter joys, thrills or special moments.

The road will not always be smooth; in fact, throughout our travels, we will encounter many challenges. If on the journey we are equipped with the proper tools and paraphernalia we can reach the ultimate destination. This book will be the powerful guidepost on your enigmatic journey. It will motivate you to change yourself for the better. As you turn the pages of this wonderful, dynamic book, the transformation you are seeking will begin its inevitable process. Anger, fear, irritation – all these negative forces which have been holding you back will find a thankful release and there will be an upsurge of positive forces. Living in the Now, sharing and caring, singing the Name Divine will find a home in your heart and take you to a higher plane of existence. A feeling of great determination to face life with all its vicissitudes will fill your being.

An incident from the life of Swami Vivekananda is worth mentioning here.

One day, as Swamiji was coming out of the temple of Mother Durga in Varanasi, he was surrounded by a large number of chattering monkeys. They seemed to be threatening him. Swamiji did not want them to catch hold of him, so he started running away. But the monkeys chased him. An old *sannyasin* was there, watching those monkeys. He called out to Swamiji, 'Stop! Face the brutes!' Swamiji stopped. He turned around and faced the monkeys. At once, they ran away. Swamiji later said: 'Always turn around and face the situation. Never think of running away.'

Face life with courage and move on with faith and fortitude. It is easy to get lost in the web of day-to-day life. You need to be aware of whither you wish to go. Take a firm hold on your life. Get into the driver's seat and start shifting the gears. Take on the challenge. Steer your vehicle in the right direction. Instead of fretting and fuming, undertake the journey joyfully. Your destination awaits you!

J. P. Vaswani

Chapter 1

Where are You Heading?

Where are You Heading?

If someone were to ask you, "What does life mean to you?" What would be your response?

When asked this question, most of us close our eyes for a brief moment and plunge into thought. We are unable to answer right away; and after a vague random sentence or two, we honestly reply with a sigh, "Actually, I don't know."

Life means something different to different people; happy people will view life very differently from unhappy people. By the same token, busy, active, working people will view life differently from reflective, contemplative or meditative people.

Many people think that life is meant to be lived for others; while some are apt to imagine that life must be lived on their own terms. Is life then all about being useful — making every moment worthwhile?

For some, life is an enigma, a painful mystery. But as they grapple with pain and suffering, even they come to realise that though life may seem cruel and unfair, it actually works.

Sometimes it's the difference between them and others that bothers people a great deal. They tend to look at life through their own narrow viewpoint — and think that all others are crazy and insane, because they don't share those views.

Some of us are horrified by the hatred and the violence around us. Rashly, we jump to the conclusion that life is meaningless.

We are born here on earth and life is to be lived in a fitting way. Wouldn't you agree?

Are you getting the best out of your bargain with life? Have you indeed made the most of your life? Are you living your precious human life meaningfully, consciously, purposefully?

I know that the answer to that question is not easy! But you will agree with me that we need to think about it, at least occasionally.

True, we all love life! We want to make the most of it. We long for happiness, peace and fulfillment in all that we do. But do we know the purpose of this life, the goal of this life?

Our saints and sages have said to us repeatedly: This human birth is invaluable, it is God's greatest gift to us, let us use it wisely and well.

Have you ever asked yourself as you snuggle into bed and drift into sleep: What have I done with my day today? Have I moved closer to God? Have I brought happiness to anyone? Have I spoken kind words?

I know several businessmen who will not leave their offices before the day's accounts are tallied and closed to their satisfaction. They insist that pending bills and unsettled transactions should not be carried forward to the next day. But how many of us tally our daily accounts in the book of life?

If truth were to be told, we live a life of inertia! We leave our accounts unsettled, untallied.

So many of us today are just drifting through life. We do not know where we are going; we do not even know what we want out of life. We work like machines, going through the same routine day after day. We forget that each of us is unique.

You are unique. God made you for a special purpose. Discover that special purpose. Make it your goal and once you have fixed that goal, you must keep your eyes fixed always on that goal. This is one of the secrets of making the most of life — fix your goal!

If I were to ask you right now: "What is it that you want out of life? What do you wish to achieve? Not many of you will be able to give me an answer straight away. To each of you I would say: You must fix your goal. It may be a material goal or a spiritual goal but you must fix your goal, and everyday, you must work to reach that goal!

Several years ago, a cartoon appeared in an American newspaper. It showed martians, (the inhabitants of Mars) looking at people on earth: One martian asks another, "What are those people doing on earth?" The other replies, "They are moving." "Where are they moving?" persists the first one. "They do not know where they are moving. They are just moving," is the reply.

We are just moving; we are just drifting. But if we wish to succeed, we must fix our goal! We should be able to describe our goal vividly. We should fix it in our imagination. And we should have an unswerving focus on the goal all the time.

Chapter 2
Every Breath is Precious!

Every Breath is Precious!

Many years ago, a saint of Sind emphasised the value of every breath of life, when he said, "If any one offered me the position of the President or Prime Minister in exchange for just one breath of my life, I would decline the offer, because the value of each breath is far greater than position, power, name and fame."

Let me tell you the story of a poor farmer, who inherited a small plot of land from his father. It was a tiny field, a stony tract of land. The farmer set out to plough the land, and found that the plough was obstructed by stones. Grumbling, he threw away as many stones as he could, and continued his ploughing.

The field was ploughed and sown with the crop. And still, the shiny red stones continued to lie around. The farmer would throw them at the birds or use them in his catapult to scare the birds away.

One day, as he was late in returning home, his wife brought his lunch to the field. Her eyes fell upon one of the shiny red stones, and she picked it up saying, "This stone is so beautiful! I shall take it home and give it to our daughter to play with."

"Take as many of these as you like," said the farmer. "There were dozens of them lying around, and I have thrown away many of them." But though his wife searched for them, she could not find another like the one she had picked up. So she took the stone home and gave it to her little girl.

A few days later, a wealthy jeweler passed by their house, when he caught sight of the girl playing with the shiny red stone. He stopped short in his tracks, and took the stone from the child and examined it closely. Amazed, he said to the child, "Can I see your father?"

The farmer came out of the cottage to greet the visitor. "Where did you get this stone from?" the jeweler asked him anxiously. "It is one of the rarest and most precious gems in the world! If you give me a few more like this, I shall give you a fortune in exchange! We don't find such large gems any more. You have probably hit upon an ancient buried treasure."

Can you imagine the farmer's reaction? He had thrown away all his treasure, not knowing its true worth!

Every moment, every breath of this life is precious, like the valuable gems that the farmer threw away in his ignorance.

Why is this human birth so precious? The answer is simple. It is only through the human birth that we can attain liberation. It is only through the human birth that we can rid ourselves of the burden of *karma* and break from the bond of birth-life-death-rebirth. That is why it is said that even in the heavenly world, good and noble souls yearn for this human birth. The purpose of the human birth is to work towards a higher life, the life beautiful. But sadly, many of us fritter away this life in worthless pursuits, little realising the value of that which we throw away so carelessly!

I urge you, I earnestly beseech you, be aware that every breath of life is precious! Spend every moment, every minute in the consciousness that life is a gift from God. It is only through the human birth that we can achieve self–realisation and return to God, to abide forever in *moksha*, our ultimate liberation.

I recall a valuable lesson that Gurudev Sadhu Vaswani taught me. One day the Master expressed a desire to have some fruits for breakfast. Eager to please him in every way I could, I asked him, "Gurudev, what fruit would you like to eat? Tell me and I will get it for you immediately!"

Gurudev Sadhu Vaswani looked at me and smiled. "I think I would like to eat a few cherries," he said to me.

"I will get them immediately," I said and rushed off to the market in a tearing hurry. I searched high and low, but there were no cherries to be found for love or money. Every vendor gave me the same reply, "The season for cherries is over. You will not find them now."

Tired, dispirited and crestfallen, I returned to the Master. "Forgive me Gurudev," I said to him, "try as I might, I simply could not find any cherries."

Gurudev Sadhu Vaswani said to me, "There is a season for everything. Once the season is over, we cannot avail of its benefits."

Well, you may wait for the next season. But life does not easily give us a second chance. This life has been given to us for our spiritual evolution. And now is the time to begin. If this season is over it will not come back!

Whatever is most important to us, must be done now. And the most important thing for all of us is the higher life that we seek. Therefore we should start the work now. Now is the time. Now is the right season.

Chapter 3
Unclutter Your Mind!

Unclutter Your Mind!

Today, scientists are beginning to understand the value and power of what is called 'thought energy'. They are beginning to study what our ancient rishis knew thousands of years ago. They taught their students *Jignasus* that a fundamental law of life is: "You become as you think."

I am happy that this truth has been reaffirmed in our days by influential thinkers and scientists. One of the fundamental laws of life is that `Energy follows thought'. As we think, so we become. If we fear a fall there is a possibility that we shall truly fall. To put it simply, we become what we think. Hence we should be very careful with our thoughts.

Thoughts have an inherent capacity to materialise. I thought of the sage who remarked, "That man is happy, who thinks the happiest thoughts." I have always said to my friends: Thoughts are things, thoughts are forces, thoughts are the building blocks of life. Therefore we must keep our thoughts clean. Whatever we think about, we bring about.

If we wish to be happy, we must unclutter our `house'– the house of our heart. We must throw out all the joy-killers, the negative thoughts of greed, ill will, jealousy, malice and envy. But throwing these out is not enough – we must fill our mind with happy thoughts – thoughts of purity, prayer, sympathy, service and sacrifice, love and kindness, prosperity and peace, success and victory.

We are so obsessed about external cleanliness that we tend to neglect what's on the inside, don't we? And what is inside is far more important, isn't it?

Let me tell you a story about why the inside matters more than outside...

A little black boy who was at a country fair was watching a man fill multicoloured balloons with helium gas and let them up. The balloons rose higher and higher, filled with a gas that was lighter than air.

"I bet the black balloons will not go up as high as the white ones," said the boy wistfully.

"Watch now, son," said the kind man. He blew up a black balloon and filled it with helium and let it go. It soared up just as high as the others.

"It isn't the colour of the balloon that matters," he said to the boy. "It's what's inside the balloon that really matters."

When your mind and heart are uncluttered, when they are filled with light, joy-giving thoughts, your spirit too, can soar high!

Scientists tell us that a magnetised piece of steel can lift up iron particles that weigh several times its weight; but if the same piece of steel is demagnetised, it cannot even lift so much as a feather's weight. When you unclutter your mind and cleanse your thoughts, you are magnetising your mind. You will find that confidence, hope and optimism fill your mind and you will achieve success and happiness.

When your mind is filled with negative emotions, you

become insecure and fearful. You are overcome by negative thought patterns; "I may fail," or "I may lose my money," or "People may laugh at me," and so on.

This kind of thinking weighs you down. You let opportunities and chances slip by; you are afraid to make bold moves; you begin to stagnate...

You are a precious and unique being! Your life has a purpose and a meaning. How can you allow your life to be weighed down by joy-killers?

Fill your mind with positive thoughts! But remember, positive thoughts cannot dwell in a cluttered mind, any more than a delicate plant can thrive in a closed, dark jar in a dry and dusty corner. Therefore, begin to believe in God, in the goodness of the heart, in the beauty and the order of the vast universe. Believe in the eternal truths and values upheld by our ancient scriptures – the values of *satya, dharma* and *ahimsa.* Such thoughts will help your consciousness to expand. The doors and windows of your mind will be opened, and you will feel the joyous winds of liberation blowing within!

Chapter 4
Paint the Right Pictures!

Paint the Right Pictures!

The most successful people are the people with the most interesting pictures in their minds. If you consciously paint a picture of yourself as a successful person, success will definitely come to you. But if you are convinced that you are a failure — even if you are placed in the best of circumstances, with the best of resources — you will fail! Such is the law. If you think of scarcity, scarcity will befall you. If you imagine abundance, abundance will flow into you.

Consciousness is built of three layers – the conscious, the subconscious and the super conscious. Tap the powers of the superconscious and the subconscious – and you can turn failure into success!

The conscious with which we are familiar; the conscious self that thinks, that feels, that takes decisions – this conscious self is a very tiny part of our consciousness. It is like the tip of an iceberg floating above water. The subconscious is much vaster. It is like the larger portion of an iceberg immersed inside the water. But this subconscious cannot think for itself. It cannot decide what is right and what is wrong. It has no power of decision. If you believe that you cannot achieve something, if you believe that you cannot do something, the subconscious will take up your belief. Its job is only to see that it proves your beliefs. Whatever you will believe in, your subconscious will create conditions, so that your beliefs are proved. Whatever you picture for yourself, the subconscious will only prove that picture as true.

If there is a fat man who believes that he cannot grow slim, he will never grow slim. He may go on a crash diet to reduce his weight, but when he is off guard, something will happen, the subconscious will create circumstances so that he is caught in the trap unawares and gains weight.

To achieve success you must have strong belief of success, you must paint a picture of yourself succeeding. The conscious and the subconscious must cooperate with each other to create success. Success is not produced only by the conscious self. It is done with the help of the subconscious. The subconscious is there to obey you. It is a very obedient servant who takes orders from his master. Its decisions are to be made by you. Its beliefs are to be programmed by you.

There was a servant whose master asked him to bring a few biscuits. He brought the biscuits in his hand. The master scolded him, "You stupid fellow," he exclaimed. "You must bring everything to me on a plate or a dish!" The servant said meekly, "Yes master, I will do that. It's a very simple thing after all."

Sometime later the master ordered the servant to bring his shoes. The servant promptly brought them on a plate. Enraged, the master shouted, "You stupid fellow, what are you doing?" The bewildered servant replied, "But sir, those were your instructions! I am only obeying your orders."

The subconscious is like the servant. It cannot think for itself. It cannot decide what is right and what is wrong. It can only obey. The subconscious is like the automatic pilot in an aircraft. If you set the auto-pilot to take the plane eastwards, the plane will keep on flying eastward.

It is only when you resume manual control that you can change the direction of the plane. This is what the subconscious does too. Therefore you have to be very careful of the thoughts you think, the affirmations that you make, specially at the time you fall asleep. There are tremendous potentialities open to every one of us. If only we make use of the right affirmations at the right time, we can work wonders!

Speaking to your subconscious with magnetic determination is known as affirmation. Let me pass on to you a simple rule of affirmation – whatever you wish to affirm, affirm it over and over again. First, affirm to draw the attention of your own thoughts. Then, softly re-affirm to draw the interest of your thoughts. Finally, whisper the affirmation as though you are coaxing your subconscious to cooperate. In simple words, first affirm loudly, then a little softly and lastly, in a whisper!

To give you an example, suppose you are unwell and want to make an affirmation about your health. You have visited a number of doctors who have prescribed a host of medicines which have brought no relief. You can affirm to yourself: "By God's grace, I feel better and better, every day in every way, every day in every way." Make this affirmation specially when you are about to slip into sleep, and when you are about to wake up in the morning. Repeat this affirmation, first loudly, three times, then softly, three times, and finally four times in a whisper. You will find that the subconscious will receive this order and create conditions that will restore you to good health. To make the affirmations more effective, they must be rhythmic. You must repeat the affirmation as if you were singing. Secondly, it must be positive. For instance, if you wish to give up smoking, don't say, "I shall never smoke again." Rather, tell yourself, "I have given up smoking." Affirm this, as if you have done it already, as if you are free from this habit. Positive thoughts induce magnetism; negative thoughts weaken your magnetism.

Chapter 5

Rid Yourself from the Burden of Anger

Anger is a wild fire, a forest fire which spreads from shrub to shrub, from tree to tree, consuming everything that comes its way. Anger creates a chain reaction. Someone gets mad at me; I must take it out on someone else, otherwise it will keep on seething within me. That someone else must have it out on yet someone else. And the chain reaction goes on! The fire keeps on spreading.

When we get angry, we may not harm the person with whom we are angry, but we are definitely harming ourselves. It was the Buddha who said, "Holding on to anger is like grasping a hot coal with the intent of throwing it at someone else; but however you are the one who gets burned." The Gita says: "Man is his own friend and man is his own foe." When I succumb to anger, I become my own enemy. I may not be hurting the other person, but surely I hurt myself. I throw poison into the blood stream.

When a person gets angry, he activates certain glands in the body. This leads to an outpouring of adrenaline and other stress hormones, with noticeable physical consequences. The face reddens, blood pressure increases, the voice rises to a higher pitch, and breathing becomes faster and deeper, the heart-beats become harder, the muscles of the arms and legs tighten. The body moves into an excited state.

If a man is given to anger, all these processes are repeated, again and again, and the man is surely heading towards serious health problems. The cumulative effect of the hormones, released during anger episodes can add to the risk of coronary and other life-threatening diseases, including strokes, ulcers, high blood pressure. It is, therefore, in your own interest that you learn to control — or, in any case, reduce — your anger.

Have you ever asked yourself: "What is the root cause of anger?" At the root of all anger is self-will. I wanted a particular dish for my dinner. If I find that something different has been made, I lose my temper. If only I can understand that everything happens according to the Will of God, and in the Will of God is man's highest good, I will not get angry, I will learn to accept everything. This happens through practice of daily silence. Everyday, sit in silence, explain to yourself that not a leaf stirs, except it be the Will of God though appearances may be to the contrary. Through practice, I will arrive at a stage of stability where nothing will upset me and make me angry.

There was a scientist who worked, at the turn of the century, on barometric pressures. Everyday, he would watch barometer several times and note down readings. For twenty long years, he did his work. He decided to make a record of all those readings and formulate a theory.

His maid-servant asked for a holiday and left a substitute. In the evening, as the scientist went out for his usual walk, he noted down the reading. On his return, he took the reading but could not note it down, as he found his papers missing. He asked the new maid-servant where the papers were.

"Sir," she answered, "I was cleaning your table, when I noticed all those dirty, stained sheets of paper. I burnt them in the fire and have kept new, clean sheets in return." The professor's labour of twenty long years was lost in a moment. But he did not utter one angry word. He only said, "Lord, Thy Will be done!"

Later, the professor learnt that there was a meaning of mercy in all that had happened. Some other scientist, in a distant country, had worked on the same problem and already published a book. Had the sheets not been burnt, he would have been put to a lot of unnecessary trouble in compiling the figures, arranging them, working out a theory and publishing a book which would have served no purpose, as a similar one was already in the market.

The plan of God may or may not be revealed to us. But we must never forget that there is always some hidden good in everything that happens. Therefore, let us greet every incident and accident of life with the words, "I accept!" It will, then, not be difficult for us to control our anger.

Chapter 6

Give a New Tone to Your Life

what's your
story?

Give a New Tone to Your Life

It was a philosopher with a great sense of humour, who wrote: "After God created the world, He made man and woman. Then, to keep the whole thing from collapsing, He invented humour."

When a black mood of gloom and despair creeds over you, perhaps, the best and the simplest way to ward it off is to laugh. Laughter is contagious. If someone beside you laughs, you find it difficult to suppress laughter. There is a man who has pinned to his wall pictures of people laughing heartily. Whenever he feels sad or depressed, he has but to take a look at the pictures; he cannot help but laugh, and immediately feels better.

I read of a man who rendered service to the sick in a simple way. All he had with himself was an album which cost next to nothing: it was a collection of "laughing" pictures taken from discarded newspapers and magazines. With this album, he went to patients, many of whom were in the throes of physical agony. They had not known what it was to smile, for days together. At the sight of "laughing pictures", they burst into laughter; they forgot their physical ailments for a while; they felt so very much better. Surely, this must have helped them in making a speedy recovery.

Yes, laughter is a tonic — physical, mental, spiritual. It is a dry cleaner which cleanses you from inside. It gives a new tone to your life. The day on which you have not laughed is a lost day, indeed. It was Victor Hugo who said: "Laughter is the sun that drives winter from the human face." And George Santayana said: "The young man who has not wept is a savage and the old man who has not laughed is a fool." I would suggest, "The young man who has not shed tears needs to move in the company of the lovers of God and the old man who has not laughed needs the company of the little ones."

Laughter is a medicine. It helps in building up moral muscles. It is a spiritual uplifter. When you feel sad or downcast, look at your face in a mirror. It looks so tensed, so ugly, so unlike the face you would wish to wear. The strain in the face is due to some negative emotion which is playing havoc in the mind. One way of breaking the force of the negative emotion is to relax. Relax the whole body. You will find that the last part of the body to relax is always the face: and of the face; the mouth is the last to relax. So smile and laugh! You will see how quickly the clouds vanish and you are happy again!

"Laughter," says Dr. Wilde, "provides a rhythmic movement of the abdominal muscles, gently massages the intestinal organs, improves digestion and blood circulation."

In the Harvard and Yale Universities of America and at the UCLA's Neuro-psychiatric Institute at West Los Angeles and at several other research institutions, neurobiologists and medical researchers have confirmed that smiling, laughing and cheerful expressions set in motion happy waves in the mind stuff and generate neuropeptides which re-vitalise the immunity system to prevent and fight disease. People who do not think of negative emotions of jealousy, envy, greed, are more healthy than people who live cloistered, unhappy lives.

Instead of complaining about life's frustrations, try to laugh about them. If something is so frustrating or depressing that it's ridiculous, realise that you could 'look back on it and laugh'. Think of how it will sound as a story you could tell to your friends, and then see if you can laugh about it now. With this attitude, you may also find yourself being more lighthearted and silly, giving yourself and those around you more to laugh about. Approach life in a more joyful way and you'll find you're less stressed about negative events, and you will achieve the health benefits of laughter.

Chapter 7
Do Not Let Irritation Sap Your Energy!

Do Not Let Irritation Sap Your Energy!

The greatest malady of modern life is that man permanently seems to be on a treadmill! He is on the move all the time, running, running, running – and still in the same place!

Rush, rush, rush! Executives are jet setting across the globe. Visiting the customers in Nigeria today; meeting with bankers in London tomorrow; trade conferences in Buenos Aires the day after; off to Chicago for a new collaboration afterwards ...

Hurry, hurry, hurry! Mothers are virtually on roller skates, dropping children at school, going off to work themselves, attending meetings, calling on doctors and bankers and plumbers and electricians, attending to household chores and managing servants ...

Under these circumstances, is it at all surprising that we are constantly prone to irritations and annoyances? One of my friends, who is a doctor, said to me the other day that many of his patients come to him with sudden outbreaks of high blood pressure. Outwardly they are calm, quiet, dignified individuals. But inwardly the daily frustrations and irritations of life are taking their toll on these men!

They easily feel upset, irritated, annoyed, unhappy. The driver is delayed in reporting for work – and his master is driven into a frenzy. Frenzy is fine, if it is going to bring the driver to his door at once. But he knows it cannot – so who is the loser?

Jimmy Durante, the comedian, schooled himself never to be upset, never to feel irritated. Whenever he was faced with a trying situation, he would exclaim, "That's the situation that prevails – so what can you do about it?"

Irritations are inevitable. We are going to encounter them wherever we are, whatever we do. If we are wise and mature, we will learn to handle them without paying a heavy price in terms of frayed nerves and acute emotions.

By giving in to irritation, we allow our energy levels to drain; our efficiency drastically lowers; and we also lay ourselves open to worse problems that are sure to follow. Have you seen the comic strip where an irate driver kicks the flat tyre of his car – and then howls in pain as his foot is sprained by the kick?

A mature and wise person learns to face life's daily irritations without being upset. The trick is to snap out of irritations and recover our calm and serenity. Better still, we should learn to block out irritations altogether, by adopting a tolerant, easy going attitude towards people and events.

Rahim was the assistant manager of a hotel. A lady had checked into one of the deluxe rooms. Each time she met Rahim, she would shoot off a list of complaints and demands; she would fuss over the messages left for her, and in general made life tough for him.

Rahim had been trained at an eminent institute and obtained a diploma in Hotel Management. But he had to grit his teeth and put up with the lady, who was beginning to get on his nerves. He spoke to his mother about her one night, when he went home.

"Be patient with her, son, and send out a prayer for her when she annoys you," advised his mother, who was a wise woman. "God knows what's bothering her!"

Rahim decided to follow his mother's advise. For the next

few days, he listened patiently to the lady and attended to her complaints promptly.

A week later, she came down to settle her bill. "Please order a taxi to take me to the airport," she requested.

"I hope you found your stay pleasant and comfortable, Ma'am," Rahim said to her. "We do hope you will come back to stay with us whenever you are in this city."

To his shock, the lady burst into tears. "Oh, I hope I'll never, ever come back here," she said with a sob. "My former husband, who deserted me years ago to run away with another woman, was in the hospital, dying of cancer. He asked to see me, and I had to come here so that I could bury the bitter past and help him die in peace. But it has been too much for me! He is dead now, and I must go back and allow my own wound to heal!"

Rahim was startled to realise that while he had been battling with the petty irritation caused by her behaviour, she had been passing through a terrible emotional ordeal.

Patience is the formula which can help you black out, shut out every kind of irritation! Learn to have an objective, detached and dispassionate attitude to problems. Try to understand why some people behave as they do, and you will find that their behaviour no longer upsets you. Instead, you will find yourself sympathising with them and trying to help them in any way you could!

Granted, it is a human tendency to want to hit back at whatever – or whoever – has annoyed you. But it can be an even more satisfying experience when you control your resentment and become the master, not only over yourself, but the situation. And remember, the man who can master a situation by self-control, always wins the battles of life!

Chapter 8
Unlock the Fullness in Your Heart!

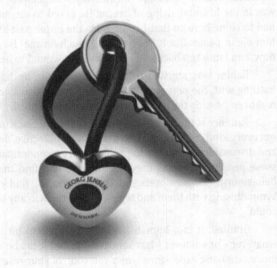

There is a fruit found in Africa, called the taste-berry. It is said that when you have eaten the berry, all else that you eat subsequently becomes sweet or pleasant to taste. Even sour or bitter food tastes good - such is the extraordinary effect of the taste-berry!

Gratitude is the taste-berry of the soul. Savour it, and you will not be subject to stress and tension.

Again and again, we try to run away from difficult situations; again and again we rebel, react with anger and bitterness. How can we ever be at peace? The answer is simple: Grow in the spirit of gratitude to God; develop the spirit of acceptance. "Not my will, but Thy Will be done, O Lord!" This must be the constant utterance on your lips.

In all conditions of life, let us thank the Lord! Let us make it a habit to praise the Lord at every step, in every round of life! In the midst of fear and frustration, worry and anxiety, depression and disappointment, let these words come out of the very depths of your heart — "Thank You, God! Thank You, God!"

Recent medical research indicates that positive emotions like love and gratitude actually enhance the immune system, which is the body's shield against attack from disease and illness. Our mental attitude and our psychological condition have a direct bearing on the immune system. Positive feelings of gratitude and joy release endorphins into the blood stream, which are the body's natural painkillers. They are said to stimulate dilation of the blood vessels and relaxation of the cardiac muscles, thus strengthening the body's capacity to resist disease and promote recovery.

On the other hand negative emotions such as anger, grief and bitterness are known to dump high levels of adrenaline in the blood. This constricts blood upon the heart. It also slows down the movement of white blood cells which fight disease and enhances our immunity.

In other words, gratitude releases happy hormones and inhibits the 'unhappy' hormones in our system thus helping us to live longer and healthier lives. Gratitude may not cure you of cancer, but it will definitely make you feel better!

How does thanksgiving heal and strengthen you? When you focus on the attitude of gratitude, you focus on all that is good and positive in your life. As all that is good and positive emanates from God, the person who practises the therapy of thanksgiving allows the most positive and powerful forces in the world to flow into him, and draws strength and healing therefrom. It is in fact, akin to being connected with a powerful spiritual dynamo.

Whenever you happen to feel tired, dispirited, discouraged and unable to cope, just thank the Lord for being there with you. You will find that your unhappy, negative thoughts drain away, and the energy of God flows into you, to make you positive and whole!

The expression of gratitude is a rich and positive exercise. It is a mental and spiritual tonic. When you allow your thankfulness to be expressed, you are affirming God's goodness and grace. Dwelling on the attitude of gratitude makes us open and receptive to the Lord's blessings. And we find that good things come to pass in our life.

Have you had a bad day? Thank the Lord its over – thank Him for helping you cope with it while it lasted. When we do this, defeats are turned to victories, as we imbibe strength from our struggles.

Acceptance in the spirit of gratitude unlocks the fullness in our lives. It can turn despair into faith, strife into harmony, chaos into order, and confusion into clear understanding. It restores peace into our hearts and helps us to look forward to the morrow in the faith that God is always with us!

When we thank the Lord all the time, we build for ourselves a ladder of consciousness on which we can climb and reach the very pinnacle of peace.

Chapter 9
Stamp Out Stress!

Stamp Out Stress!

Have you seen the cartoon that says:

"There are only two times I feel Stress?"
"Day and Night"

Truly, the world today is full of tension. Wherever I go, I find people are tense and nervous. Stress and tension are more common in their incidence than the common cold.

Today hospitals are full of patients who suffer from diseases due to stress. Stress is the cause of a number of physical ailments. Stress keeps on accumulating in the minds of the people until, one day, it manifests itself in the form of one ailment or the other.

What is this "Stress" that we are talking about? It is a much-used, much misused term. Dr. Hars Seyle, expert on stress-management, tells us: "Stress is the wear and tear on your body caused by life's events." It is the sum total of the body's physical, mental and chemical reactions to circumstances which cause fear, irritation, worry, anxiety and excitement.

There are hundreds of experiences in our everyday life which cause stress. These stress-causing events are called stressors. These stressors can create good stress (positive stress) or distress (negative stress). Normally, our body and its systems are conditioned to cope with stressors. But there is an optimum level at which each one of us can cope with stress and still function well. When the limit is exceeded, we become victims of stress.

Stress originates from a French word which means constriction or delimitation. It is true that stressful situations seem to squeeze us, limit our emotions and reactions. Stress therefore, is regarded as a potential killer. It saps one's energy and undermines one's well-being.

Stress is purely subjective. What is a stressful situation for one person, may be child's play for another. For instance, if a person is asked to say a few words to a large gathering, he may panic and lose his nerve completely. A fluent public speaker, on the other hand, would regard it as an opportunity, and end up speaking for a long time!

Stress has been known to have a snowballing effect. It keeps accumulating unless tackled or treated effectively.

Stress Busters To Eradicate Stress From The Human Psyche

Stress Buster No. 1

Revamp your attitude to a positive one.

The workplace becomes akin to a jungle when situations and people get out of hand but our attitude can always be within our control and it can be a positive one.

Following are the steps to cultivate a positive attitude:

- Set aside time everyday to replenish your mind with positively charged thoughts.

- Whenever you feel you are gripped by negativity,

fall back on some dynamic and inspiring thought from any scripture that appeals to you.

Unhappy and dejected, the amateur writer gave up hope of finding a publisher to print his work. In a moment of madness he threw his draft into the dustbin. Finding the abandoned manuscript in the basket, his wife picked it up and placed it before him, "My dear Norman, you cannot give up! Your work will get noticed and will surely be appreciated."

The author was Norman Vincent Peale and ironically the book was, "The Power of Positive Thinking", which turned out to be an inspirational, best seller.

Stress Buster No. 2

Work in the consciousness of the present moment.

When challenges stare at us, we are so overwhelmed by their sheer impact that we analyse its past and predict its effects on the future. It is important that we deal with the problem in the present moment consciousness. This helps to tackle the problem in a practical way.

Most of our lives are wasted either feeling guilty about the past or worrying about the future. Trying to be in another time zone whilst physically being present in the now is a big stressor.

Schedule your activities in "day-tight compartments", which means to plan reasonably achievable goals within the framework of the day. Then completely focus only on those targets without thinking about jobs that are not planned for that day.

Stress Buster No. 3

Try praise and appreciation, for a change…

- Use praise generously and sincerely.
- Thank colleagues and subordinates for every little thing they do. There is no better motivator.
- Maintain a gratitude journal. Each day allot time to write a list of all the blessings and bounties that you have been taking for granted.
- Once you have developed a habit of being grateful, your focus will always be on the positive, thereby activating the law of attraction to fill your world with joy and plenty.

Stress Buster No. 4

Streamline your life.

Simplify and streamline everything from the workplace to the home front.

At the workplace, delegate well, communicate efficiently and use time management!

Unclutter your mind as well as the space around you.

Organise your work load to make it simple. Organise chores and errands at home on a priority basis. All this, once done in a systematic way, will reduce stress.

Chapter 10
Welcome to the Now!

Welcome to the Now!

A simpleton was walking along the street when he was lost in deep thought. He was thinking about how he had escaped from a fire just a day earlier. So lost was he in thought that he began visualising the scene as he stopped on the street. He frantically waved his hands to and fro. People laughed at his predicament but no one realised that they too live either in the past or the future.

Watching this a holy man approached him with a ring. It had an inscription which said, "Welcome to the Now". The holy man kept repeating it again and again. "Welcome to the Now". We all need to program our minds every time we slip away from the present, "Welcome to the Now".

Life is here and now! We all know that life is often compared to a book, each chapter representing one particular phase of our life; but there is one major difference between my life and my book; I cannot turn back the pages of my life! I cannot revisit the past! Nor can I read the final chapter of my life before its due time. Life has to be lived in the present!

There were two sisters who were travelling by long distance train from Jammu to Kanyakumari. Due to adverse weather conditions, the train halted at a station in central India, until conditions improved, and the tracks were cleared. The passengers were stuck on the train for hours together.

The elder sister was annoyed, irritated and frustrated; she railed and ranted; she complained bitterly to the TTE and the conductors, who were helpless themselves; she sulked endlessly and became a source of annoyance to all her fellow travellers.

The younger sister on the other hand, refused to allow her spirits to be dampened by the delay. She went around cheerfully, making friends with the others, exchanging jokes, playing with children, starting singing sessions in different carriages, conducting quiz contests to keep young people occupied, and generally spreading good cheer all around. Strangers responded to her, sharing their food with her, inviting her to join their group, and enthusiastically joining her efforts to 'organise' games for the entertainment of all.

When the train finally reached its destination, the elder sister was morose, depressed and tired. She felt that her time had been wasted. As for the younger sister, she had had the time of her life! She had made so many new friends, she had had such new experiences, and she had managed to retain her good mood and her good humour all along. She had enjoyed the journey, despite the delays and the setbacks and all the little inconveniences. She had made the most of the present.

Living in the present maximises all the possibilities that life offers to us. We are able to focus on what is happening around us and savour all those little joys and pleasures that are available in the here-and-now.

The past is over and done with; the future is in God's hands; the best that anyone can do is to live in the present, wisely and well. As the proverb says, "Sufficient unto the day is the evil thereof." In other words, the day will have its own share of challenges, difficulties, rewards and achievements; why should we complicate matters by dragging our regrets of the past and fears of the future into the present?

The trouble with most of us is, we hardly ever dwell on the happy experiences that we have had in the past. Most of us seem to harbour a permanent love affair with the sorrows and regrets and failures of the past! We hug these bitter memories to ourselves constantly, refusing to let go of the bitter past. In a beautiful sonnet on the theme of remembrance, Shakespeare compares this attitude to repaying old debts that have already been settled long ago!

Imagine that you have taken a housing loan, and have paid it off diligently over a period of years. After the whole thing is over, will you keep transferring money to your loan account just because you like to dwell on your own past? Is that not futile and foolish, apart from being a waste of your money? So why dwell on past memories that are negative and bitter? This too, is emotional waste of a high order!

The past is over and done. The future is yet to come. What is real, is the present moment. Let us make the best use of the present. Let us make it beautiful.

Chapter 11
Be Yourself!

Be Yourself!

M an, as they say, is a social animal. We live in society, and therefore, it is necessary that we observe certain norms and social obligations. It has rightly been said that there is nobody in the world who knows everything. It is equally true that we can learn something or the other from everyone we meet. By all means respect other people's views and attitudes. Keep an open mind that is receptive to other people's ideas – but do not become a slave to other people's judgements.

Many people live under constant stress, trying to 'keep up appearances' as the saying goes. "What will the neighbours think if I walk to work?" "What will my friends say if I don't give a party?" "What will the society say if I don't arrange a grand wedding reception for my daughter?" and so on.

I must confess I am amused at this supposedly rhetorical question, "What will people say ...?" My answer is always this – don't bother about what other people say! Let them say what they like. But do not let them upset you. What other people say does not really matter; it does not really count in the ultimate analysis. What really matters, what counts is what you do. Do your duty. Say to yourself again and again, "They say: what do they say? Let them say."

Modern psychology emphasises that an individual should develop a healthy self-image. Ask yourself: should your self-image be based on what others want, what others say, and what others expect? Should others set the standards for where you live, how you live, what car you drive and what clothes you wear? Such a life would indeed be intolerable to any thinking person.

I heard a few years ago that many young women in the West were falling victim to an eating disorder called anorexia nervosa – in their anxiety to stay pencil-slim in imitation of models and film stars, they began to eat less and less, until they could not even stand the thought of food.

How sad it is when people are not comfortable with how they look, how they talk or how they walk! They are always comparing themselves unfavourably with others – they are constantly wishing that they could be different. "If only I could be like her...", "If I had his dress sense...", "If I were as tall as you...", such people are not happy with what God has made them to be! They do not like themselves, and so they live by the likes and dislikes of others. They try to gain the approval of others; they try to please others in order to feel good about themselves.

Mr. and Mrs. Kapoor were celebrating their tenth wedding anniversary. "It's your day today, honey," Mr. Kapoor said to his wife lovingly. "We will go wherever you want and do whatever you want!"

"Do you really mean that?" Mrs. Kapoor demanded. "Will you take me wherever I want to go?"

"Sure, just state your wish – and it shall be my command," her husband assured her playfully.

"In that case," she said, "I would like to go to a five star hotel for dinner tonight."

Her kind and generous husband agreed. True, the outing was going to be very expensive; but after all it was their tenth anniversary. He would do his best, and more – to make his wife happy.

It was the first time that the couple were eating out at a five star restaurant. The ambience, the decoration, the luxury of the place was indeed breathtaking! The waiters treated them like royalty. Mr. Kapoor was really enjoying the experience.

However, Mrs. Kapoor seemed to be labouring under considerable stress. She constantly kept looking over her shoulder. Everytime the door opened and someone entered the restaurant, she would almost jump out of her skin and scan their faces eagerly. While her husband was thoroughly enjoying the delicious and expensive dishes placed before them, she was hardly aware of what she ate!

The lavish meal came to an end. "It's the best ice cream that I have ever had," Mr. Kapoor exclaimed with satisfaction, as he paid the bill, adding a generous tip for the waiter. "In fact, it's the best meal I've ever had, don't you agree, honey? I must thank you, for making this experience possible. After all, it was your decision to come here."

Mrs. Kapoor was looking dejected and downcast. It looked as if she would burst into tears any moment. "What's the matter, dear?" enquired Mr. Kapoor anxiously. "Is it that the food hasn't agreed with you? Why, you look ill! Are you sure you are alright?"

Mrs. Kapoor was trying to blink back her tears. "It's so unfair," she said to him with a low sob. "We've spent two thousand rupees to eat at this place, and none of our friends have seen us here! Of what use is it, if they don't know we are dining at a five star restaurant? What a waste the whole thing is!"

This is what living by others' standards can do to you. You end up living a life of pretence and hypocrisy. You are wearing a mask, you 'put on' a face or an attitude to impress other people – and you cease to be true to yourself.

Chapter 12
Overcome Your Fears

Overcome Your Fears

Fear is a poison that quickly circulates through the entire system, paralysing the will, producing a queer sensation in some part or the other of the human body. Fear is a great foe of man. And fear is a merciless master.

Why is it that the vast majority of us live perpetually in fear of something or the other? Perhaps, one reason is that we are lonely. The deepest tragedy of the modern man is his loneliness. In spite of an ever-increasing number of clubs and cinemas, museums and parks, hotels and restaurants, at heart we feel so lonely.

A distinguished visitor to America was taken to a big cinema-house. Throngs of people stood in rows awaiting their turn to get a ticket. Asked for his opinion, the visitor said:

"The Americans must be very lonely at heart; else there would not be endless queues at cinema-houses!"

Yes, if we will confess the truth to ourselves we will not deny that we feel lonely. We lack the security of protection. We are like the child who, taken to a fair, lost its mother in the crowd, with this difference that the child rents the air with its cries for the mother, "Ma! Ma!", but we have forgotten even to cry for our Divine Mother. We are like the orphan who was never tired of complaining that there was no one to care for him in this big, boisterous world. It is this sense of loneliness that leads to a feeling of frustration, and so many of us do not find it worthwhile to live in the world. Not long ago, a multi-millionaire brought an end to his life after leaving a brief note on his writing-table: "I feel lonely. Therefore, I kill myself!"

We feel lonely; we feel lost; we feel abandoned; we feel forsaken and forlorn. Again and again, we lose the sense of security which belongs to us as children of God; we fall into the abyss of fear.

Overcome fear the moment it appears or it will overpower you. Strike fear with the weapon of the Spirit — the word of God. Utter the sacred Name dear to you, the Name of the Beloved: Krishna, Shyama, Rama, Jesus, Buddha, Nanak. Utter it, again and again. Utter it in child-like faith, and He whom you call will rush to your aid. Say aloud some prayer which has an appeal to your heart. Not unoften I repeat the prayer from one of Gurudev Sadhu Vaswani's songs:

> Thy sea is vast, my skiff is small:
> I trust in Thee, who guardest all!

Recite these or other lines which may appeal to you; recite them, again and again, until fear departs and you feel strong as steel.

I can never forget the sweet, serene face of a child I saw sixty years ago. I was on board the S. S. Versova, travelling from Bombay to Karachi. Suddenly, a terrible storm arose. Thick clouds appeared in the skies, covering the face of the sun, and the day became dark as night. Huge waves lashed against the steamer which tossed as a paper-boat. All the passengers were filled with terror. It looked as though we were doomed to a watery grave. In the midst of this sorrowful scene sat a little child, barely six years old — calm, serene, undisturbed by the shrieking storm and the rolling wave.

I marvelled at this child's unruffled serenity in the face of death. I said to him: "The steamer is about to sink; are you not afraid?"

With a cherubic smile he answered: "What have I to fear when my mother is near?"

I can never forget those words. When in the depths of despair and sorrow I have repeated the words to myself, repeated them again and again, I have felt relieved — "What have I to fear when my Mother is near?"

Our Mother, the Mother Divine, is so near to each one of us. Closer is She than breathing and nearer than hands and feet. Alas! We have turned our faces away from Her. In our shouts and shows, our engagements and occupation, our business and commerce, we have forgotten Her. We have lost the child-like spirit. We need to become children again, friendly and loving towards all, not critical, never fearful.

Chapter 13
Never Mind — Let Go!

Never Mind — Let Go!

Betrayal, hurt, anger, disappointment — sometime or the other, we have to face these negative emotions in our life. When we dwell on other people's rudeness and insensitivity, we walk into the trap of bitterness and negativism. You constantly think about your disappointment, and then you begin to talk about it and you are trapped in resentment.

How best can we face such disappointments and frustrations? You can choose to react differently, by taking responsibility for your own emotions and feelings. You do this in the full awareness that others do not 'cause' your feelings. You choose your own.

It may be a cliché to say that it is useless to cry over spilt milk. But it's only too true. We have to learn to let go of disappointments and get on with our life. We need to forgive.

This is especially difficult when other people don't seek our forgiveness, or indeed when they are clearly in the wrong and don't deserve to be forgiven.

Never mind — let go!

In such situations, forgiveness allows you to let go of a no-win situation and walk out of it unhurt, unscarred by bitterness.

People alas, are not perfect. At home, at work, people are going to hurt you or let you down at one time or another. If we remain in charge of our feelings, if we are in control of ourselves, we can be two steps ahead of the situation. We will not be victims of circumstances.

Let me give you a small exercise. Think of two people who have hurt you, made you angry or let you down recently — two people about whom you still feel animosity.

Now ask yourself: What is my animosity doing to me? Do I feel happy holding on to it? Does it make me feel happier? Does it improve my sleep? Is my life better, richer, more meaningful because of my resentment?

If the answer to all the above questions is NO — then take a courageous decision.

Let go! Walk away from the disappointment and the bitterness!

A girl came to a holy man and said, "I know not why, but I am unable to sit in silence and pray or meditate. I feel restless. I used to be so happy."

The holy man asked, "How is it?"

The girl answered, "I think it has something to do with one whom, at one time, I regarded as a friend. But she was very cruel to me, and I said that I would never forgive her, never talk to her. I am sorry I said it, but since then there has been no peace in my heart. What shall I do?"

The holy man said, "It is better to break a bad vow than to keep it. Go to her and seek her forgiveness."

The next morning, she went to her friend and confessed her uncharitable attitude and asked her forgiveness. The one whose forgiveness was sought burst into tears.

She said, "You have come to ask for forgiveness. It is I

who should be asking for forgiveness, for I am ashamed of my wrong attitude."

The two friends were reconciled.

To arrive at forgiveness, one has to pass through four stages.

The first is the stage of hurt. Someone has wronged me, done something mean to me. Someone has been unfair to me and I cannot forget it. I feel hurt. The hurt keeps on throbbing within me. It is here that we must remember that it is not I who feels hurt, but the ego.

Hurt leads to hate, which is the second stage. I cannot forget how much I have been hurt and I cannot send out thoughts of goodwill to my enemy. In some cases, I hate the person so much that I want him or her to suffer, as much as I am suffering.

Then comes the third stage of healing. God's grace descends on me and I begin to see the person who has hurt me in a new light. I begin to understand his or her difficulty. My memory is healed and I am free again.

Then comes the fourth stage of coming together. I am anxious to make friends with the person who hurt me; I invite him into my life. I share my love with him and we both move to a new and healed relationship.

To choose to let go of resentments is to walk the way that leads to a life of freedom and fulfillment.

Chapter 14
Create Heaven Within

so simple that often its importance is overlooked. But it is one of immense value to us all.

Are our homes breaking? Is our unity crumbling? Are nations at war with each other? The cure of these and other ills is *kirtan.* O pilgrims on the Path! Get together and form *Kirtan* – bands. You will sanctify your own lives; you will purify, as did Sri Chaitanya centuries ago, the atmosphere of your town and country; you will release forces for the healing of the human race.

2. As you wake up in the morning, breathe out an aspiration of purity, of love, of joy, of peace, of humility, of trust — any aspiration that may express inner most need. Repeat this aspiration as often as you can during the day, even in the midst of your work.

3. As you retire at night, read a little from the life or teaching of a saint, a *bhakta,* a man of God. This has a purifying influence on the mind and consequently, on one's dream-consciousness.

4. When evil thoughts come to you, do not struggle with them. The more you struggle, the more you strengthen them. The best way to face evil thoughts is to let them alone and to think Divine thoughts. Light dispels darkness. Every good thought is as a ray of light which clears the dark clouds of evil thoughts.

5. Keep yourself relaxed at all times — both in body and in mind. So work with un-hasting speed and speak gently, sweetly, in love and understanding. And let nothing disturb your inner peace. Imagine the world as an ocean in which stormy waves rise high, threatening to drown you: be still and full of trust in the Lord of the ocean. The waves will pass away. In all difficulties and dangers, believe with the ancient seer who exclaimed: "All is well, a thousand times well, both now and a million years hence!"

Chapter 15
Love and Give and Share!

Love and Give and Share!

One day, as I was walking through the solitude of the woods, I recalled the sacred words spoken by my Beloved Master, Sadhu Vaswani, "Life is brief. Our stay upon this earth is but for a few days."

People tend to forget that life is ephemeral. Sometimes, I think they do not realise that they themselves are mortal! They speak and act as if they will live forever; they want to possess things — possess things permanently! They cling to their possessions as if they own them for eternity. People are so obsessed with their belongings, their houses, their cars and all their wealth that they do not want to part with them at any cost. I see many families around, bitterly divided over property matters. They fight with bitterness over their share of land, houses and other possessions. An advocate once told me that several pieces of prime real estate in Pune, worth hundreds of crores of rupees are lying vacant and disused because the members of the family are involved in bitter court battles lasting for years!

I knew of two brothers, one of whom lived in the US, while the other lived in India. The brothers had a dispute over the family property. The younger brother decided to go to the US to settle the dispute and to claim his legitimate share. But alas, on the very day he reached the US, he breathed his last. This man perhaps carried within his heart, the weight of years of bitterness and anxiety. The discord between the two brothers had hurt both of them. The conflict served no purpose. In fact, one of them left this earth disgruntled and unhappy.

Property is a sacred trust given by God; it must be used to fulfill God's purposes. No person has absolute or exclusive control over his or her possessions. The concept that people have only custodial care of the earth, as opposed to ownership, is illustrated by this Hebrew story:

Two men were fighting over a piece of land. Each claimed ownership and bolstered his claim with apparent proof. To resolve their differences, they agreed to put their case before the rabbi. The rabbi listened but could come to no decision because both seemed to be right. Finally he said, "Since I cannot decide to whom this land belongs, let us ask the land." He put his ear to the ground and, after a moment, straightened up. "Gentlemen, the land says it belongs to neither of you but that you belong to it."

Leo Tolstoy the great Russian writer has said, "When two brothers fight over the property and want to divide it, God above laughs, for all land is His, and our life is too short to be wasted in bitterness and hatred."

People often put a question to me, "What is the purpose of our life if we are supposed to live without our wealth and possessions?" Others want to know, "Why should we not fight for what legitimately belongs to us? That would be only fair and just."

True, you must claim what you think is your own, as long as it does not break homes, bifurcate families and bring disharmony and turbulence in life. For the aim of life is to cultivate the soul and to experience peace and bliss. One important element of living is to love unconditionally. For love without sacrifice has no meaning.

Most people live life on the surface. They live a superficial life, unaware of the goal or the meaning of their life. This life, as I said earlier, is given to us not to possess and own, but to love and give and share whatever we have with those less fortunate than we are. Life is too short; why should we waste our precious time in conflicts, quarrels and court cases? Instead, we should patch up all our differences and live in harmony with one another, for time is running out for all of us. Death can claim us at anytime; and then, it may be too late.

Chapter 16
Bring a Glow in Someone's Heart

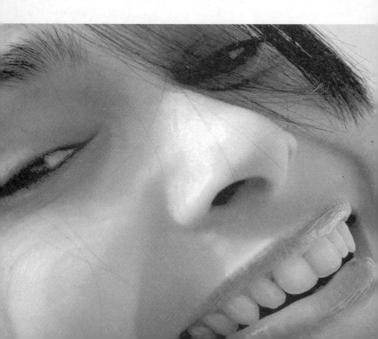

Bring a Glow in Someone's Heart

The American philosopher William James; tells us: "The deepest principle of human nature is the craving to be appreciated."

Human relationships thrive on caring, sharing and mutual appreciation. We rely on our loved ones, our friends and those closest to us, for moral support and encouragement, don't we?

The amazing thing is that appreciation costs us nothing, It requires hardly any effort. A smile, a warm gesture, a word of praise is all it takes; and yet we are so reluctant to offer it to others.

Is it not true that all of us feel happy when we are appreciated? In this, as in other things, what we send comes back to us. For life is like a boomerang: what we are, what we do, comes back to us. When we give our best to the world, when we send out warmth, love and appreciation — it all comes back to us.

Of a great English poet, I read that he never spoke a word of appreciation to his wife. As long as she lived he criticised her and found fault in everything that she did. Suddenly, the wife died. The poet was grief-stricken. He was ashamed that he failed to write poems in appreciation of her, when she had been alive. "If only I had known," he lamented. "If only I had known....."

Truly it has been said, life is too short to be small. Let

us not be small-minded. Let us be generous with praise, appreciation and encouragement.

There was a distinguished American surgeon who was also kind-hearted and generous. His heart was touched by the little crippled boy at the street corner, from whom he bought his daily newspaper. He was always smiling and cheerful and the surgeon decided to operate him and help him walk and run and play like other boys of his age.

He made arrangements with the local medical school for the boy's surgery. The hospital which was part of the medical school offered all its facilities free of cost for the operation – if the medical students would be allowed to witness the operation and learn from the great surgeon.

The surgeon explained to the boy what he planned to do, and the boy agreed happily. He thought that it would be wonderful if young medical students learnt from the surgeon – for they would be able to help many more crippled children like him.

The day of surgery dawned. The boy was wheeled in the operation theatre and placed on the operating table before the surgeon and his assistants. A little away from the group, behind glass partitions, students were seated in rows as in a theatre to witness the procedure on closed circuit TV.

The doctor began by talking about the boy's condition and the procedure he was about to follow. When the preliminary talk was over, he turned to the little boy who lay on the table, a little anxious, a little afraid and a little excited. "Now Johnny, we are going to set your leg right," he said to the boy kindly, as the anesthetist got ready to put him to sleep. The little boy raised his head and said in a soft, clear voice, "Doctor, I think

Live Not for Self Alone!

A cold wind was howling and rains beating down heavily, when the telephone rang at the residence of a rural doctor.

The doctor struggled awake and saw the bedside clock. It was 12.30 am!

The doctor was a kind and compassionate soul. He picked up the phone and enquired who was calling.

"It's my wife!" cried the farmer who called. "She needs a doctor right away. Can you please come at once?"

"Sure, I'll come," said the doctor. "But can you come and get me? You see, my car is being repaired."

"What?" sputtered the voice on the line. "How do you expect me to come out on a night like this?"

The trouble with us is we always expect goods and services — but we are unwilling to give it ourselves.

"I am doing nothing but giving," grumbled an irritated man. "I am tired of giving."

"All right, let's make a deal," his guardian angel said to him. "You stop giving the moment God stops giving to you!"

Give, give, give! That which you give in the Love of God for the service of the poor and broken ones, the forsaken ones, the forlorn — that is credited to your account in the Bank of Heaven.

Giving his young son a ten dollar bill, a rich father said, "You can do whatever you like with this money!"

Later in the day, he asked the child, "What have you done with the money? Did you spend it well?"

"Yes," said the child. "I lent it to someone."

"Did you make sure about the security of your loan?" enquired the anxious father.

"Yes," replied the boy. "I gave it to a man who looked very hungry."

"That was foolish of you. Now you will probably never get the money back."

"But Dad, we were told in the church that what we give to the poor is a loan to the Lord Himself."

Touched by his son's simple faith, the father reached into his pocket.

"Here is another ten dollar bill for you, son," he said.

"There!" said the boy. "I was sure I'd get it back. Only, I didn't know it would come so soon!

Share what you have with others, and you will be richer in material and spiritual terms. Compassion does not require a hefty wallet, strong limbs or heroic deeds or great and austere sacrifices. A helping hand, a friendly word or gesture, a kind smile will more than suffice. We do not always have to give money — we can always give of ourselves.

Pandit Omkarnath Thakur was visiting the holy city of Haridwar – one of the greatest pilgrimage centres for

Hindus in India. As he walked down the banks of the holy River Ganga, the great classical music exponent saw a blind musician, desperately trying to play his dilruba.

The Pandit noted that the man's palm was badly injured, which was why he was unable to play the instrument.

"Can I help you, my friend?" he asked gently.

"I am in such a fix," said the blind man. "The pilgrims pay me some money if I play my instrument. Now, I have hurt myself and I cannot play. It looks as if I will have to starve today!"

"May I try to play your dilruba, my friend?" enquired the Pandit. "It seems to me you have a fine instrument!"

"It is, brother," said the blind man with great enthusiasm. "My father made it for me specially! But do you know how to play it?"

"I can try," said the great musician. He began to play so beautifully, that before long, a huge appreciative crowd had gathered before them. People showered coins and notes on to the white cloth spread before the blind man.

When the old man had gathered all the money happily, Panditji slipped away quietly.

When we learn to move away from the obsession of the self, from brooding on ourselves and our wants, when we come out of ourselves and learn to care for others, our fears and anxieties will vanish like mist before the rising sun. Live for others and not for self alone.

Chapter 18
Make Spirituality a Reality!

Make Spirituality a Reality!

Spirituality does not mean turning your back on life; it is not renunciation or asceticism; it is not running away from the problems of life. It is the source of courage and inner strength that will enable you to take on life's challenges in the awareness that you are a spark of Divinity; that within you is a *shakti* that is of the Infinite!

Gurudev Sadhu Vaswani often said to us, "You are not a weakling, as some of you imagine yourself to be. In you is a hidden *shakti,* an energy that is of Eternity." The Gita tells us too, that man is not the body he wears, but essentially the Spirit, the *atman* within.

An enormous treasure of *shakti* lies locked and hidden within us. But we go through life, without ever unfolding this *shakti* without using it for our own betterment. Little do we realise that we have the hidden potential that can transform our lives. There is a Powerhouse within us and yet we live in a state of permanent power failure!

The question is: How can we awaken this *shakti*? How can we connect with the soul? How can we promote our spiritual well-being? You can get this strength by appealing to the Supreme *Shakti,* the All-Powerful, the Almighty. Seek His strength. Appeal to Him, "O Supreme *Shakti,* give me strength."

Make this Supreme Divine Power real in your daily life. Make this Infinite *Shakti* your senior partner in life. We have confined God to the Sanctum Santorum of our temples and shrines. We have locked up the Great Universal Divine Power behind golden and silver facades. Let us make God real for ourselves! Walk on the pathway of life, do your allotted work, live and move and breathe in the awareness of His Omnipresence. Remind yourself of the fact that He is constantly watching you, watching over your every activity. You will discover that your tasks are easily done and your wishes are fulfilled and your problems are solved.

You are a spark of the Supreme Self. You are a child of God. His power and energy are yours. And you can harness this tremendous spiritual energy through self-disipline, by connecting to God through *sadhana.*

Do not wait for old age to begin to practise your spirituality! The happiest men and women are those who fuse, integrate spirituality into their daily life. Make God a reality in your life. Make Him a friend, a partner, a guide, a guardian, a parent, and invite Him to watch over all that you do.

The purpose of your life is to cultivate the soul. Hence, even while you are attending to your work, stay connected to the Source of all life; stay in constant touch with God. If you are able to set aside personal time, spend some of that valuable time in any form of *sadhana* that appeals to you. This will help you achieve the kind of inner peace and bliss that work can never bring to you.

Spend a little time in prayer, in introspection and in silent communion with God. Realise the value of the present moment – the here and the now. Realise that this moment is God's greatest gift to you. Begin now, to chant the Name Divine!

Do not live for yourself alone, for that will make life small and selfish. Learn to live for others and you will find that life blooms like a beautiful flower! The day on which you have not helped a brother here, a sister there to lift the load on the rough road of life, is a lost day indeed!

True spirituality is not a matter of indoctrination. It cannot be inspired by compulsion. You are free to enquire into its principles — you must be convinced of their truth, before you accept them. The laws of life are inviolable; they need no defenders, no patrons and no protectors. Each one of us must reach the Highest by his own free choice. This is the great truth taught to us in the ancient scriptures of India.

In the Gita, after Lord Krishna passes on many truths concerning life to His dear devoted disciple Arjuna, He finally tells him: "I have declared the truths to you; you must go and reflect upon these teachings and do as you choose."

The choice is yours!

Chapter 19
Speak Nothing but the Truth!

Speak Nothing but the Truth!

Satyaat nasti paro dharma.....

There is no religion higher than truth. This is the injunction laid upon us by the ancient scriptures of India. Truth is the very first step that the seeker has to take on the path to salvation. Truth is dear to God, and dear to men of God.

A shopkeeper who ran a busy grocery store, decided to try an experiment. He wanted to know how many of his customers were really honest.

So, one day, he decided to give excess change to everyone who did his shopping at his store.

The amounts he gave away were not really large. To some, he gave a rupee or two in excess; to others seventy or eighty paise; to a few, he gave five or ten rupees more than they had to receive.

The results of the "experiment" were revealing, indeed! Out of a total of 33 people who came to his shop, 8 customers simply pocketed the change he gave them. They were trusting souls, they did not even bother to check if he had given them the right change.

Another 8 out of 33, counted their change; and on finding more than their due, they drew his attention to the mistake and promptly returned the extra money to him.

More than half of all the customers — 17 out of 33 — checked the money that was given back to them; found that it was more and quietly pocketed the excess and walked away from the shop!

To which class would you belong?

There is an incident from Gandhiji's childhood, narrated to us in his autobiography. Once, a British Inspector of Schools visited Gandhiji's school. Such visits were meant to check the proper functioning of the school and appraise the teaching-learning programme offered to the students. The inspector decided to give a surprise spelling test to the children in Gandhiji's class. He read out five words from the English text and asked the children to write them down correctly. One of the words was 'kettle', and Gandhiji mis-spelt the word. The teacher, who saw the mistake, whispered to Gandhiji to copy the correct spelling from the slate of the boy sitting next to him. Gandhiji understood what was happening; but he could not bring himself to copy from another. He retained the wrong spelling, and was pulled up by the inspector, as he was the only boy who had got the word wrong! To Gandhi, truth was more valuable than silver or gold!

Undoubtedly we will face great difficulties in our quest for truth; but the man of Divine qualities overcomes them by his perseverance on the path. Many of us, alas, give up the effort. "It is an impossible ideal to put into practice," we assert. "It is not just unattainable, it is impractical," we lament. There are many excuses people offer for not adhering to the truth: we are afraid that the truth will hurt us and our chances of advancement and success;

we use untruth as an excuse to cover up our deficiencies. It is only a man of courage who can stand up to the test of truth at all times in his life. Such is the value of truth that attainment to the Supreme Soul, the Almighty, is referred to as *sat-chit-ananda* or true, eternal bliss of awareness. We also have the much revered concept of *Satyam, Shivam, Sundaram* — the embodiment of truth, goodness and beauty that is Lord Shiva.

If you wish to tread the path of truth, become aware of why you do not speak the truth. Is it out of fear? Or is it due to desire for gain? Or perhaps, out of ill-will and the wish to hurt others? Address the root cause, and do not let negative emotions like fear, greed and ill-will dictate your attitude. When you conquer these negative emotions, you learn to speak the truth in utter freedom. Do not rehearse half-truths or lies as excuses to utter to friends: if there has been a lapse on your part, admit the truth. Not just outright lies, but also exaggerations and omissions amount to falsehood: therefore, in all important matters, learn to speak the truth, the whole truth and nothing but the truth. Remember that gossip, slander and rumour are some of the worst forms of falsehood. Refrain from these at all times, and at all costs. Practice honesty in all your transactions, especially when they relate to money matters. Avoid malpractices in all business dealings.

To travel the path of truth is not only difficult; it needs a tremendous amount of discipline, courage, steadfastness and determination. But the rewards of following this path are spectacular and most important, eternal.

Chapter 20
Chase away the Evil Thoughts!

Chase away the Evil Thoughts!

In an early hour of the dawn, I sat in my quiet room. My eyes were closed; my mind was at rest; and in the depths of my soul, I held a conversation with the Beloved. I felt inexpressibly happy.

Suddenly, as a swarm of locusts swoops upon a field, undesirable thoughts attacked me from all sides. I felt disturbed, distracted, distraught. Only a moment ago, I bathed in the Pure Ganges of God's presence: suddenly I found myself wallowing in mire and mud. I could no longer sit silent. My mind became restless as a drunken ape.

I left my room. If only to change surroundings, I proceeded to the garden. My heart leapt, as from a distance I saw, sitting on a bench underneath a tree, him whom I revere as my Master. I went and sat at his feet. Within me a storm raged.

The Master sat in silence. His eyes were half-closed, resting on the Far-Away. He was the very picture of the Peace that defies description. I gazed and gazed and still gazed at his face. Out of it flowed an influence which seemed to soothe my distracted mind.

After a while, the Master opened his eyes; his gracious gaze fell upon me. He smiled and asked: "What ails you, my child? You seem to carry a great load on your mind."

"That is true, Master!" I said. And I spoke to him of all that had happened as I sat in silence in my little room.

And I said; "Master! Whence come these evil thoughts in the face of which I feel helpless as a mouse in the paws of a cat? And what may I do to check the restlessness of my mind?"

The Master gave an understanding smile. And he said, "My child! Do not feel worried! Let the evil thoughts come: let them come out! The more they come out, the purer will your mind become!"

Astonished, I asked, "Do the evil thoughts come out of my mind? I always felt they came to me from somewhere outside!"

"Nay, child!" the Master said. "There is in you a depth you do not know. The well you see in front of you is very deep, but deeper than the well is the depth within you. In it lie stored the *samskaras* of many births. For birth after birth have you taken and garment after garment have you shed before taking on your present human body."

"Is there then absolutely no hope?" I asked. "Can I do nothing to check the restlessness of my wandering mind?"

"There always is immense, hope" the Master said. "For within you is the Power, the *shakti* of the *Atman* (the Spirit)."

"These be difficult things to understand," I said. "Speak to me, Master! Of some simple discipline which I may follow to keep the mind from wandering."

"The simplest way," the Master said, "is repetition of the Holy Name. My experience has taught me that three Names are specially efficacious — the Names of Krishna and Nanak and Isa (Jesus). But other Names, too, must be equally helpful. Of Abu Said, the Sufi saint, we read that he sat in a corner of his room and continually repeated for seven years the Name, 'Allah! Allah! Allah!' And he became a new man, a holy man sought by hundreds of seekers on the Path."

After a brief silence, the Master asked me to clap my hands. I obeyed. At the sound of the clapping, the birds sitting on the tree flew away.

"See how the birds fly away at the clapping of your hands," the Master said. "So do the birds of evil thoughts fly away as you clap your hands and sing the Name of God. Sing the Name as often as you can. And as you sing, meditate on the form or some symbol of the Great One whose Name you sing. Sing it in love and longing for the Lord. Sing it with tears in your eyes. Sing it aloud. Sing it in the silence of your room or as you walk on the street. Sing it alone or in the company of other *bhaktas*. And evil thoughts will disturb you no longer."

"But, Master! One cannot sing the Name all day long!" I said.

And the master said, "Sing the Name till you can sing it no longer. And let the rest of your time be spent in desireless activity devoted to the well-being of all creatures. Work for the good of others, but see that your work is free from all taint of egoism. Work as an instrument of the Eternal, knowing that He is the One Worker! Such work will purify you and prepare you for a life of contemplation.

Chapter 21
Chat with Your Best Friend!

Chat with Your Best Friend!

Today, many friends who are separated by distance, ensure their contact is kept alive by constant 'chat' sessions and 'text' messages as they are called. God is the Friend of all friends. When all other friends fade away, He is the one friend who will remain. But how do you get in touch with Him? He is available to us twenty-four hours of the day and night, seven days a week, three hundred and sixty five days a year. He is ever ready to help us. How can we seek His help?

Prayer is the swiftest and surest way to establish a link with God. It cleanses your thoughts, purifies your mind and elevates your consciousness. It enables you to talk to God directly and much more effectively than you can to people. For you can be sure that God listens carefully to every word you say!

You do not need a cellphone or a bluetooth device to contact God! You need to be attuned, 'in sync' as they say, with the still, small voice that is heard deep within your heart.

In the beginning, we do not hear His voice; but let us be sure that He hears us! We may not see Him; but He sees us. And ultimately a stage comes in the life of every seeker when he sees God and hears His voice. For God can be seen; He can be touched and felt; His voice can be heard. He is more real than all things which we perceive with the senses. But to be able to see Him and hear Him, effort is needed. This effort is to awaken deep longing, yearning for God. So it was that Sri Ramakrishna said, "Yearn for God even as a miser yearns for gold, as a lover for his beloved, as a drowning person yearns for a breath of air!"

It is not necessary for us to offer set prayers. Prayer should flow spontaneously out of a love-filled heart. One look of the eye, one exclamation, may be more acceptable to the Lord than hundreds of set prayers offered in a mechanical way, day after day. Feeling is needed; emotion is needed. For, more important than the words, is the vibration of love which they carry.

God does not care for the form, the shape, the vocabulary of our prayer. It is the feeling that counts.

A poor farmer, returning home from the market after a long tiring day, found that the wheel of his cart was about to come loose. He was in the middle of the woods, and his cart was loaded with produce.

Anxiously, he searched his pockets for the little prayer book, which he always carried with him. To his dismay, he found that he had forgotten to bring it with him.

He closed his eyes and began to pray thus, "Dear God, I have done something very foolish. I have left my prayer book at home, and my memory is not what it used to be. I don't seem to remember a single prayer. So this is what I am going to do. I shall recite the alphabet — very very slowly — several times. Since You know all the prayers, please put the letters together and form the right prayer for me!"

The Lord said, "This prayer is the best I have heard today - for it came from a heart that is simple, pure and sincere!"

It was William Law who said, "God does not care for the arithmetic of our prayers, how many they are. He does not care for the rhetoric of our prayers, how eloquent they may be; nor the geometry of our prayers, how long they be; nor the music of our prayers how melodious they are; nor the logic of our prayers however argumentative they may be; nor the method of our prayers, how orderly they be. But the sincerity and fervency of our prayers — how heartfelt they are."

Opening your heart to God is the most effective form of prayer. I urge my friends never, ever to forget their "daily appointment with God", as I call it — a brief, simple prayer first thing when you get up and a quiet, reflective prayer before you fall asleep at night. Therefore, let us not miss our daily appointment with God. We take care to keep our appointments with clients, suppliers, business associates, and also with our doctors, dentists, bankers and lawyers. More important than all these is our daily appointment with Our Best Friend. Let us never fail to keep it! You may utter prayers from the scriptures; or use your own words when you pray. The language of the heart is the best for any prayer!

Chapter 22
Cast Your Cares!

Cast Your Cares!

He was a singer of God's Name. As he sang, he filled the hall with the rich melody of his voice and he thrilled the hearts of his listeners with the richer music of his dedicated life. With outstretched arms, he sang, again and again:

> Behold!
> The birds do not sow
> Nor do they reap:
> And they save not
> For the morrow.
> Yet each day
> They eat and drink
> To their fill,
> And lift up their hearts
> In gratitude to Him who is
> The giver of all that is!
> O ye that would tread the pilgrim-path!
> Cast all thy cares upon the Lord!
> Chant His Name,
> By day and night:
> And fill the Earth
> With the fragrance of Heaven!
> He, the Lord of Love,
> Becometh, in love,
> A server and a burden-bearer
> Of His devotees
> And their disciples!

The words summed up the secret of his own life. He toiled not, nor did he have any bank-accounts. He asked for nothing, and he lacked nothing. And his needs were supplied in a mysterious way.

More than once he came to our *satsang* (fellowship meetings) and did *kirtan* (singing God's Name). We listened to him with rapt attention; we joined in his singing; and the eyes of many glistened with unbidden tears.

On one such occasion, as the *kirtan* came to a close, an elderly gentleman, who sat near me, asked: - "How does he manage to live? He never asks for anything of anyone!"

And I said to him, "Does a prince need to beg of anyone? His Father, the King, gives him all he needs — and more!"

My elderly friend did not grasp the meaning of my words. He smiled a bland smile.

My thoughts were elsewhere. I recalled how, on more than one occasion, Sri Ramkrishna, speaking to his disciples, said, "The man of faith is like a python. He moves not in search of food; his food comes to him."

There was a woman of ninety. She never felt upset over anything. She was never tensed, always serene and tranquil as the waters of a lake on a windless day, always at peace with God, with those around her and with herself.

Someone asked her how she could be serene in all conditions and circumstances of life. She answered, "I think it is because I become a little child every night."

"What is meant by that?" she was asked.

She answered, "Every night, I go to my silence corner. I look at my Beloved, Lord Krishna. I place all my worries and anxieties and problems of the day, one by one, at His Lotus Feet. If I am feeling guilty about something I have done — I might have inadvertently hurt or caused grief to someone — I ask for His forgiveness and then accept it. If I am worried about anything, I hand over the problems to Him and let go of it. If I feel lonely or unwanted, I tell Him so and He enfolds me in His loving arms. Always, after letting go, a deep peace settles over me and tensions disappear."

Today, I wish to say this to you, "Why have you clung to your burdens all these years? Drop them! Cast all your cares upon the Lord! Throw all your burdens at His Lotus Feet. And feel for once the joy of living!"

God is the Absolute Truth, the Supreme Power. Repose faith in Him and watch miracles happen in your daily life!

Bond with Him, communicate with Him, establish a direct, personal link to Him. Keep your daily appointment with Him. Talk to Him. Make Him the source of your life-energy. Build a strong and intimate rapport with Him. Make Him your Guide – Call out to Him constantly, "O Saviour, protect me, O Giver of Life! Guard my every step! O My loving Father, abide with me!" You will never ever be alone, as long as He is with you, in your heart.

Our problems and difficulties begin the moment we cease to be 'children' in spirit — children of God. When I think I have grown up and I am able to look after myself, I am faced with trials and tribulations which overwhelm me again and again, and which rob me of the joy of living.

I had met a young college student some time ago. "Life is like a maze, a riddle," he complained. "I feel confused, confounded. I see no way out of the perplexities and problems which baffle me again and again. I feel like a child who has lost his way in a huge fair. What do you think I should do?"

I said to him, "Was there a time in your life when you were really not confused or worried?"

"Yes," he laughed bitterly. "It was probably when I was one-and-a-half years old. And I hardly remember it now, but I know I had a happy, carefree childhood!"

"Exactly," I said to him. "If I become a child, I do not have to worry. The child trusts its mother and knows that the mother will always keep it safe from harm."

"You too, can become a child," I continued. "For that matter, so can all of us. All we need to do is hand ourselves over to the Lord— and He will take care of everything."

Don't be totally worried about everything that's going around you. It's my job.

Signed,
God

Chapter 23
Set Yourself Free!

Set Yourself Free!

Sri Ramakrishna Paramhansa was brilliant at illustrating the most profound and complex truths of life by means of beautiful and simple parables. One day he said to his disciples, "Everyday, fishermen cast their wide nets into the sea. A few fish are caught in the net. Many escape. Those that have escaped the net, swim about freely in the ocean; indeed, some fish are never ever caught. But those that are caught in the net, struggle to escape; and some of them actually succeed. They leap so valiantly, that they free themselves from the net, and get back into the vast and deep waters of the sea, where lies their true home. There are other fish caught in the net who also struggle to be free – but in vain. In vain they seek a way out, for someone to free them from the death-trap that ensnares them. They struggle persistently.

"But there are a few fish who are blissfully ignorant, happily unaware of their condition. They are content to rest passively in the net that ensnares them, unaware of the terrible and painful fate that awaits them."

In this significant parable, Sri Ramakrishna refers to the human condition; especially to the four kinds of people in the world – the *nityamukta,* those who are not touched by the bonds of *Karma;* the *mukta,* those who, through their own efforts and the grace of God, liberate themselves from the bonds of *karma,* third, those who seek liberation and are struggling for it constantly; fourth, those who are so entrapped in their worldly life that they are unaware of their own bondage and seek nothing.

Let us not waste our efforts in trying to figure out complicated issues such as population growth and the fate of new souls. The question that should concern us is: What should we do, what can we do to liberate ourselves from the bonds of *karma?* We are imprisoned by the *karmic* bonds of our previous births, so much so that they have become the shackles of our present existence. We carry the yoke of negative *karmas* and we long to break free, like the pathetic fish caught in the nets of the trawler.

Don't let anyone tell you that escape from the snare is impossible! Liberation is yours for the asking. You can make your life anew. For man is not a creature of his destiny. He is the creator of his destiny.

It is not necessary to destroy *karma*. In destroying *karma*, we may be sowing new *karma*, which we will have to reap in a future existence.

What is necessary is to destroy the sense of doership. What binds me is not *karma*, but the thought that I am doing *karma*. It is the false sense of ego which keeps me bound mercilessly to the wheel of birth and death, the wheel of suffering and pain. The way to be free is to renounce the sense of doership — "I am not doing anything; things are being done through me. I am but an instrument of the Will Divine."

When man becomes an instrument of God's Will, he is liberated from bondage to *karma*. This is possible through self-surrender.

When I surrender myself to God, my false ego vanishes as mist before the rising sun. Then I know that I am not doing – I cannot do – anything on my own. The supreme Will of God is working in and through me.

A distinguished visitor arrived at a quarry where poor labourers were toiling hard. He went up to a few of them and asked just one question of each man, "What are you doing?"

The first one snarled angrily, "Can't you see I am breaking stones?"

The second one wiped the sweat off his brow and replied, "I am earning a living to feed my wife and children."

The third man looked up at him and said cheerfully, "I am helping to build a beautiful temple!"

You can imagine which one of the three men was creating good *karma* — although all of them were doing the same job!

George Macdonald said, "I find that doing my duty - doing the Will of God — leaves me no time for disputing His plans!"

Another name for doing God's Will is 'duty'. Duty simply means concentrating on what is God's Will for us now.

As Sri Krishna unfolds His doctrine of *karma* in the Gita, the very first thing He insists on is devotion to one's duty. "Do your duty, O Arjuna!" says the Lord. The name given in the Gita for duty is *swadharma.* But the Lord lays down the most important condition when He insists on detachment:

Seek to perform your duty; but do not lay claim to its fruits. Be you not the producer of the fruits of *karma...* (Chapter 2, *shloka* 47)

Herein lies the secret of the turning point in our lives. In itself *karma* is not evil; it becomes evil when it is mixed up with desire. Verily, desire-tainted action leads continually to the wheel of birth and death. Even those who seek the heaven-world, says Sri Krishna, are slaves of desire.

Therefore, we must not seek the fruits of performing our *swadharma.* He who does not desire the fruits of his *karma* is the conqueror of desire! Freedom from desire is the ultimate freedom.

Chapter 24
Make Satsang Your Precedence

Make Satsang Your Precedence

We live in an uncertain world. The only certainty in this world of uncertainty is that every passing day, every fleeting moment draws us closer to the day when death will come and knock on the door and exclaim, "Vacate the house." The body will then drop down but we shall continue to live in the life that is undying. Are we prepared to face death with courage and equanimity? Have we made the necessary preparations to face our Creator? Have we made ourselves ready for the life after death?

May I tell you, dear friends, that our life – a little interlude in this world – is part of a Great Design. It is a training ground for self-growth. Very few of us are aware of this purpose. But it is definite that our sojourn on this earth is predestined – perhaps by our own choice – for this life has been given to us for our own spiritual progress and evolution. However, we spend our life in the pursuit of pleasure, thinking that it is the be-all and end-all of our existence. We are so enamoured by the superficial glamour and glitter around us, that we forget the very purpose for which we have come. Daily attendance at the *satsang* will ensure that we do not throw our precious life away in such frivolous pursuits.

Very often when we ask people why they are not attending *satsang* regularly, the reply is, "There is no time" or "I am busy with my work" or "I do not even get time to take a deep breath..." and so on. Such excuses cannot fool anyone, not even the people who make these excuses! Some people even say, "Well, when I retire from my active job, I will definitely devote my time to *satsang,* spiritual pursuits and God." But such a time rarely comes.

When we return home in the evening, we have several options before us. We can go to the club or to the gym; to a theatre or a cinema hall for our entertainment. We may become the proverbial couch potato staring all evening at what we ourselves call the idiot box! But some of us choose *satsang* above all these options!

Satsang is a place of hope and serenity; it is a place of positive vibrations, which protects us from the negativity of the world. The temptations of the world are many and the allurement of the world is powerful. Anytime it can drag us into the whirlwind of pleasure, pelf, worry.

Let me tell you, when we go to the *satsang* we are sure to earn our own reward! We can imbibe the teachings of the holy ones, ponder over the sacred words of the scriptures, internalise the spiritual values and bear witness to the teachings of the great ones. Then for sure, our life will be filled with the peace and joy we so earnestly seek!

Satsang has a positive effect on man. *Satsang* creates pure and positive vibrations which neutralise the negative emotions of man. Recently, I was told about a young girl who attended *satsang* regularly. She was popular and respected at work. She had a great ego. She was under the wrong notion that she was influential and could exercise her authority over other *satsangis.* This girl was also adamant and strong willed; if anyone disobeyed her she would shout and scream. Many obeyed her for the fear of being scolded.

When this came to the Guru's notice, he said, "Her attending *satsang* is a waste of time. She hasn't learnt anything from the teachings of the *satsang*."

Attending a *satsang* is not enough. You have to learn the essence of its spirit. You have to imbibe its truth. When you do so, *satsang* brings about a transformation in you. This transformation is seen in many ways. A man of *satsang* is kind and humble. He is a man who readily offers his service to others. He tries his best to mitigate the suffering of the others. He lends a helping hand, whenever and wherever needed.

Man's life is so crowded with mundane activities, that he rarely has time for self-study and introspection. He seldom finds himself in that expansive, tranquil mood of silence and reflection, where he can listen to God, and chant the Name Divine in the heart within. It is said that the worldly desires are like the salty waters of the sea. Such waters can never quench man's thirst. On the contrary, his thirst increases and his craving for fresh water grows even more acute!

The message of every *satsang* is 'go within'. Go within! Explore your interior world and you will find that Divine Light which dispels every darkness! When a man falls ill he goes to the hospital to be treated. Even so, when man realises that he is falling a prey to evil, he should go to *satsang*. *Satsang* is like the hospital, which will treat the disease called 'evil'.

Satsang creates pure and beautiful vibrations, wherein you can experience immense peace and harmony within.

Chapter 25
Be Inwardly Detached

Be Inwardly Detached

Life is like the rainbow – a multicoloured, multisplendoured thing, in which the joy of sunshine and the tears of rainfall are both reflected equally. Conditions are not always to our liking. When we are placed in such adverse conditions, we must accept them and rise above them with patience and fortitude. There is a simple *mantra* which will help us pass through the most adverse circumstances with a smile: This too shall pass!

Life does not come to us with a special warranty. Change, as they say, is the only constant in life. Given this kind of uncertainty, the wise ones amongst us imbibe the valuable lesson that in this transient, impermanent life, everything passes away, sooner or later. That is why our sages and saints gave us the *mantra:* "This too shall pass away."

A father took his four-year-old son to a fair. The child wore his best dress and was careful to see that it did not get spoilt.

Suddenly, a cyclist dashed against the child who fell down and hurt his elbow. The father picked up the sobbing child in his loving arm and, with a handkerchief, covered his bleeding arm.

The child cried all the more. And the father said to him, "You are a good child and the elbow has not been very badly hurt. It will soon be healed."

"Father, I am not crying over the elbow!" the son exclaimed. "I am crying over the shirt which has been torn. The elbow will be healed, but not the shirt."

"But isn't that wonderful?" said the father. "Suppose your elbow were like your shirt and would never heal?"

The son began to see things in a new light.

"O, yes," he said, "If the elbow were like the shirt, it would never heal. God has made us in a special way."

And the smile reappeared on his tear-stained face.

We need to remind ourselves of this great truth that God has made us in a special way. We are so obsessed, overcome by the material world of *maya* that we fail to realise this Divinity within us. Material things cannot be compared to the Life Eternal. All things will pass away. Therefore, develop the spirit of detachment. Attend to your duties – but be inwardly detached, knowing that nothing, nobody belongs to you. You are only an actor – and also a spectator – in the ever-unfolding, cosmic drama of life.

Grow in the spirit of surrender to God and the Guru. "Not my will, but Thy Will be done!" Let me be the first to warn you, this is rather difficult to practise. There is always a conflict between 'my' will and God's Will. I may want to go in one direction, but God may pull me and show me another direction. This not only causes conflict but it causes frustration. Hence, to avoid this state of frustration we should learn to cultivate the spirit of detachment, and accept the Will of God. By accepting God's Will in a spirit of detachment, we will escape from the vicious cycle of desire-disappointment-frustration-pain, and *acquire* the spirit of contentment. We will begin to experience the *peace* that passeth, indeed surpasseth understanding.

Wisdom consists in accepting God's Will — not with despair or resignation, but in peace and faith, knowing that our journey through life has been perfectly planned by Infinite love and Infinite wisdom. There can be no mistake in God's Plan for us! There is a meaning of mercy in all that happens to us, for God is all love and all wisdom. He is too loving to punish us. He is too wise to make a mistake. Therefore, if something comes to me that is contrary to my personal will, I must accept it as the Will of God. As Gurudev Sadhu Vaswani taught us, "Every disappointment is His appointment."

Chapter 26
Build the Connection Upward!

Build the Connection Upward!

It's a hectic life that we all lead! We all have our duties to attend to. We have several obligations to fulfill. We cannot retire to the *tapobana* or the forest of meditation, as the holy men did in the dim, distant past. We have to live in this world, we have to carry out worldly duties. But while we attend to our duties sincerely, faithfully, honestly, earnestly, let us also carry the consciousness of God within our minds all the time.

"Seek ye first the Kingdom of God," the Bible tells us, "and all these things shall be added unto you."

A holy man was invited to visit the estate of a wealthy landowner. As evening approached, the rich man took the visitor to the spacious terrace atop his mansion and pointed to each direction.

"Do you see those orchards to the East? I grow apples, pears, plums and peaches there. As far as the eyes can see, the orchards are mine!

"Do you see the farmland that stretches to your West? I grow potatoes, cauliflowers and cabbage in those fields. Fifty percent of the State's supply comes from my lands!

"Do you see those beautiful gardens to the South? I am growing exquisite flowers for export out there. There are dahlias, chrysanthemums, roses and lilies. My gardens stretch for miles in that direction.

"Do you see those virgin forests to the North? They belong to me, too! There are millions worth of the country's best timber out there — teak, rosewood, oak and pine — they are all mine!

"I have worked hard over the last 30 years and built up this green treasure and it is mine, on merit!"

He waved his hands all over, turning triumphantly in all directions. "It's mine and I own all that you see in any direction from my home!"

He paused, searching the holy man's face for some reaction, expecting words of praise, admiration and appreciation.

The holy man laid his hand upon the wealthy landowner's shoulder and pointed upward. "Tell me brother," he said gently, "how much do you own in that direction?"

We are told that on an average, over 300,000 people die every day — men, women and children. Does it not make you wonder, when my turn will come, when your turn will come? We all know that we have arrived here on this earth with a return ticket. Back to our true Homeland, we must all return sooner or later. Therefore I say, let the thought of God be in your consciousness all the time!

If you receive all that the world has to offer and you have not got God, you have gained nothing. To get nearer to God, one should develop deep longing in the heart within. This is possible through sitting in silence and growing in the spirit of humility.

There is a beautiful story told to us in the Mahabharata. It is said that the God of the Ocean once said to the River Ganga, "O Ganga! You bring with you huge banyan and oak trees as you flow into me.

Why is it that you don't bring me some of those tender, delicate herbs that grow on your banks?"

The Ganga replied, "Those tender herbs you speak of may appear frail and weak, but, even though my water sweeps over them with force, they only bow down low before me, allowing me to flow past. Oaks and banyans, on the other hand, stand up against my flood, and I break them by their roots."

Egoistic defiance will only break you. On the other hand, humility will give you the strength to resist adversity. If you bend, you cannot be broken!

Spend sometime in silence, everyday! And put to yourself the questions, again and again: What am I? Whence have I come? Where is my true Homeland? What is the purpose of my visit to the earthplane? One day, the answer will come to you out of the depths within. And to you will be revealed the Secret of Life. You will see, and you will know!

You may have a number of appointments to keep everyday. Never to forget to keep your appointment with God. Pray to Him everyday, "God guide me, bless me, use me! Make me an instrument of Thy help and healing in this world of suffering and pain!"

Chapter 27
Depend upon the Lord Alone!

Depend upon the Lord Alone!

As we proceed on the pathways of life, we face different types of weather — stormy and smooth, wild and mild. As our spiritual life unfolds, we pass through some trying experiences. We have to face difficulty and danger, ignominy and insult. Not unoften, we feel distressed and distraught – completely frustrated in mind and heart. Such experiences are not without a purpose. They teach us to turn to God, to depend upon Him for everything. "Thou alone art, O Lord! I am naught! I am weak. Be Thou my strength!"

Calling upon God for help in times of trial and tribulation may appear to some to be a very selfish act. But all our acts, in the beginning, have to be selfish – until we learn to become "spectators" and watch the drama of life unfold itself on the stage of time. If to rely upon God is to be selfish, it is far better to be "selfish" than to be "egoistic" and rely upon our own limited powers. This "selfishness" is a necessary step in our spiritual evolution and will, at the right time, drop of its own accord – even as the flower drops when the fruit is born.

The one lesson we all need to learn is – utter dependence upon God. Everything else will follow. We must learn to turn to God for every little thing we need — until, one blessed day, we find that we need nothing; our one and only need is God! When this happens, all that we need is provided for –

naturally, spontaneously, always at the right time. Before we need a thing, it is already there. Everything comes to pass at the right time in the right way. Then one moves through life like a king. When a king moves out every thing is prepared for him in advance; he does not have to ask for anything. All his needs are anticipated and provided for. Ye are kings! Why wander ye like the king's children, in the story, who starved and were clothed in rags, though around them were heaps of costly raiments and choiced foods?

We lay our trust in things which cannot trust themselves. We lay our trust in banks which fail and in bonds whose values fluctuate with every passing whim of a statesman or a dictator. We lay our trust in children and friends who do not hesitate to betray the trust, when it suits them. We lay our trust in earthly power and dominion, in abundance of worldly goods which are perishable and pass away. We do all this with a view to build up security of an uncertain life in an uncertain future. Alas! We sacrifice the security of a certain life in the certain present, which would be ours if only we place our trust in God!

When we lay our trust outside God, we bind ourselves to a life of ceaseless struggle. And struggle means uncertainty: struggle means anxiety, worry. We are tossed hither and thither like a storm-beaten boat knowing not whither we move. All our time is spent in providing for some untoward happening which need not occur at all. All our time is spent in making preparations for living, so that we really never live at all. Little wonder if our lives are bereft of the joy of living.

There is a ladder which leads to the holy height where shines the white Light of Eternity. It is the ladder of faith, of trust. Believe in God! Trust in Him completely. Know that He will always do the very best for you. Therefore, cooperate with His Will. Become a willing instrument in the Hands of God.

When man surrenders himself to God, He takes upon Himself his entire responsibility. All we need to do is to hand ourselves over, in childlike trust, to the Lord. And the Angels of God will go ahead of us to clear the way. We shall be free from fear, anxiety, worry, stress, tension. We shall find that all our needs are provided for even before we become aware of them.

Therefore, pray each day, "So bless me, Lord! That I may learn the one only lesson I need to learn – utter dependence on Thee!"

Chapter 28
Give Up Your Ego!

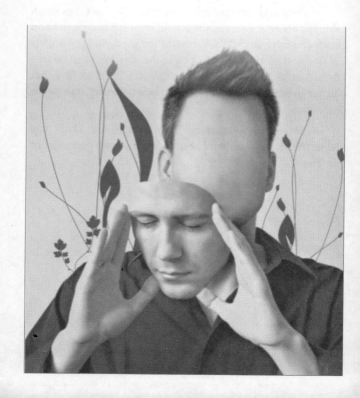

Give Up Your Ego!

Why is it that we are sometimes apt to think that God is not with us? Why do we feel lonely and helpless? If God is an ocean of love and He is always with us why does He allow us to doubt His Love and His Divine Power? Why do we experience this feeling of being abandoned and orphaned? The reason is, that there is an invisible veil between God and us. It is the veil of the self, the veil of the ego.

Gurudev Sadhu Vaswani often said, "When the ego goes, God glows." If only you would erase the ego, you will see God. Gurudev Sadhu Vaswani always assured us that it was easy to find Him, for He is nearest to us. In this connection, he quoted a saint, "Learn the art of vanquishing the ego." Give up your ego. Forget yourself and you will realise God.

Once a great king decided to renounce his power and possessions and seek initiation from Gautama the Buddha to be a monk. The entire assembly of *bhikkhus* had gathered around the hermitage to witness this royal initiation ceremony.

The king arrived, dressed in an ochre robe. His head was shaven, and he had dispensed with all his ornaments. He walked with bare feet through the assembly of monks – and in his right hand, he carried a priceless diamond, as an offering to the Master. In his left hand, he carried a rare and beautiful white lotus – in case the Buddha refused to accept the ostentatious offering of the diamond.

The Buddha, seated with closed eyes, said to the king, "Drop it!"

The king, aware of the unsuitability of the offering,

immediately dropped the diamond. Buddha's voice commanded again, "Drop it!"

This time the king dropped the lotus.

Again the voice commanded, "Drop it!"

The king was baffled, for he had nothing to drop now. He continued to walk towards the Master. But the Buddha said once again, "I say to you, drop it!"

The king understood. In one of Buddha's discourses, he had heard the Master say, *"yena tyajasi tam tyaja"* – Leave that (the ego or the I thought) through which you have left everything!"

He understood that he was still in the grip of the ego; he was still entertaining the thought that he had dropped the diamond and lotus at the Master's command.

At that moment, he surrendered himself totally to the Buddha and dropped his ego. The Master opened his eyes and acknowledged him with approval – for at that moment, the king had surrendered himself truly.

Once, a question was put to Gurudev Sadhu Vaswani, "What is true knowledge, the absolute knowledge, the greatest wisdom?" Gurudev Sadhu Vaswani replied, "True knowledge is the realisation that I am nothing, He is everything. This realisation makes man humble and gentle. And there is no wisdom greater than this."

During his European tour, Gurudev Sadhu Vaswani visited Paris. There he was taken to see Napoleon's Memorial. Napoleon was a great General, who became the de facto 'emperor' of France and he conquered many nations. Gurudev Sadhu Vaswani said later, "When I stood by the grave of this great soldier, my eyes shed tears. The ruler of the great empire was just a fistful of dust. O man, do not be proud, one day you too will be just a fistful of dust."

Gurudev often said to us, "The hum of humility is humiliation." If anyone criticises you, if anyone degrades you, if anyone hurts you, then consider yourself to be lucky. Accept the harsh words of criticism and humiliation, because he lightens the burden of your ego."

One day Buddha was walking through a village. A very angry and rude young man came up and began insulting him. "You have no right teaching others," he shouted. "You are as stupid as everyone else. You are nothing but a fake."

Buddha was not upset by these insults. Instead he asked the young man "Tell me, if you buy a gift for someone, and that person does not take it, to whom does the gift belong?"

The man was surprised to be asked such a strange question and answered, "It would belong to me, because I bought the gift."

The Buddha smiled and said, "That is correct. And it is exactly the same with your anger. If you become angry with me and I do not get insulted, then the anger falls back on you. You are then the only one who becomes unhappy, not me. All you have done is hurt yourself."

"If you want to stop hurting yourself, you must get rid of your anger and become loving instead. When you hate others, you yourself become unhappy. But when you love others, everyone is happy."

The young man listened closely to these wise words of the Buddha. "You are right, O Enlightened One," he said. "Please teach me the path of love. I wish to become your follower."

The Buddha answered kindly, "Of course. I teach anyone who truly wants to learn. Come with me."

If you want to grow in the beauty of the Higher Life, then accept criticism and praise in the same spirit, and you will be richly blessed!

Chapter 29

Escape from the Turmoil of Life!

Escape from the Turmoil of Life!

All physical, mental and intellectual effort uses up energy. To make good this loss, we require repose. Even as night follows day, rest and relaxation must follow stress and effort. Of course, restful sleep at night is vital for our well-being. But apart from this, I recommend strongly, the practice of silence during the day.

We live in a world where everyone talks far too much! We talk excessively in public and in private. As a wise man said, "Men seem to feel the need to cloak and excuse their imperfections and wrong deeds in a mass of prattle." We need to devote a few minutes each day to the healing, soothing, purifying influence of silence.

Silence is relaxation for the mind, even as rest is relaxation for the body. It should be our earnest effort, at least once a day, to escape from the stress, strain, tension and turmoil of life, and practice absolute silence. We can easily give up mindless activities like watching TV or gossiping with friends, to devote to the practice of silence.

Silence helps us commune with the inner Self, silence enables us to discipline our petty, calculating intellect. Silence takes us close to God. In silence, we can feel our prayers reach Him and in perfectly held silence we may even hear His answers to our prayer!

I call my habitual hours of silence, my "daily appointment

with God". It is vital that we cultivate the healing habit of silence in this age of noise and ceaseless activity. In fact, the great need of modern man is silence. To help us to avoid stress and tension, the noted psychologist, Deborah Bright, recommends what she calls PQT — Personal Quiet Time – of twenty minutes, twice a day.

Even as particles of dust cling to our clothes, so too, particles of noise cling to our hearts. To clean our clothes, we wash them with soap and water. Even so, to cleanse our soul we need to take a dip in the waters of silence every day.

Silence heals, silence soothes, silence comforts, silence purifies and silence revitalises us. In this world of allurements and entanglements, the sharp arrows of desire, craving, animal appetite, of passion and pride, of ignorance, hatred and greed, wound our souls again and again. Our souls bear the scars of many wounds. Silence is the great healer that can heal these wounds.

We must remember that silence is two-fold. There is the outer silence; it is absence of noise, freedom from the shouts and tumults of daily life. And there is interior silence; it is freedom from the clamour of desires, the cessation of mental acrobatics, the stilling of the play of conflicting forces. It is the peace that passeth, surpasseth understanding. Not until we have reached this peace, can we hope to experience unbroken joy and harmony for which our distracted hearts, minds and souls cry out constantly.

The powerful effect of the spirit on the body is generally recognised today. As I have stressed repeatedly, the body cannot be healthy if the soul is sick. Therefore, we may conclude that if we wish to be healthy, we also have to be 'holy'.

Do not be alarmed by that word 'holy'. It does not really mean what you think — pious and devout to a fault. The word 'holy' comes from the Anglo-Saxon root "wholth" meaning the entire being. Spiritual harmony is absolutely vital to combat the physical disharmony that we call disease. Spiritual harmony is best cultivated by the practice of silence.

When we shut out the harsh and grating noises of the world — the deafening sound of men, machines, automobiles, strife, arguments and clashes — our hearts and minds are quietened, and we listen to the Divine harmony within us. It is of this Divine harmony that Shakespeare writes:

> Such harmony is in immortal souls;
> But while this muddy vesture of decay doth grossly
> Close it in,
> We cannot hear it.

Beautiful and serene is the silence of the spirit! When we enter its realm, we experience peace, harmony and a sense of well-being. Our ego gives way to Divine love. Our stress and tension melt away. In this condition, we can listen to our inner voice which can help us solve the most difficult problems of this life.

Chapter 30

Make Me! Mould Me! Shape Me!

Make Me! Mould Me! Shape Me!

We are told that when Michelangelo saw a barren rock or an abandoned slab of marble, he could see the vision of the beautiful figure which could be carved out of the inert mass of stone. But two things are necessary to make the imagined, beautiful sculpture, a reality. The first is to choose the right piece of marble; the second is an expert sculptor. And the piece of marble must be entrusted to the care of the sculptor, to be carved and chiseled at his will.

The true disciple must cleanse and purify himself and hand himself over to his Master, to shape, mould and make him into an image of the Divine!

One essential mark of the true disciple is implicit obedience to the Guru's wishes. "Not my will, but the Guru's will be done," says the true disciple at every step. And the more he is attuned to the Guru's will, the more he will grow in the likeness of the Guru, until, one blessed day, the disciple becomes a part of the Guru's being. The disciple flows into the Guru; the Guru flows into the disciple. The twain are one, one in the One who is Peace, Joy and Bliss!

But, obedience must come from within; and it is born out of three important attributes: faith, respect and devotion. These are the foundation of obedience. When we have Guru who can kindle these attributes in us, it is easy for us t practise obedience.

The Guru does not need outer acts of reverence from you. What matters to him most, is your inner attitude of reverence and devotion in acts of obedience. For this culminates in self-realisation. Obedience has but one meaning — to obey. I may deliver a hundred discourses on obedience, and write multiple volumes on the subject — but, I have not advanced a single step, if I have not learnt to obey. The way of obedience is that which leads to the way of surrender, of which the Gita speaks in such rapturous terms.

We can differentiate between two types of obedience that the Guru asks of us – passive obedience and dynamic obedience. Passive obedience is what most of us try to practise with regard to the laws and rules of the state that are imposed on us externally. More often than not, we 'obey' them out of fear of fines or imprisonment, etc. On the other hand, dynamic obedience comes from within. We do it of our own volition, without external compulsion, for the sake of our own spiritual progress. In the more mature stages of discipleship, this obedience becomes second nature to us — it is 'internalised' to use a term from modern psychology. Dynamic obedience is the sign of the disciple's evolution and maturity. It is a sign of his true *sadhana* – of self-discipline and conquest of the ego.

As we progress on the path of obedience, we tend to become less argumentative, less questioning. It is not that we become passive; it is just that we are more intuitive, and therefore arguments and questions become futile. We understand the Guru better and find it easier to merge our will in his. Our entire awareness is focussed on the Guru. The

Guru's word is final — there are no questions to be asked, no compromises to be made, no alternatives to choose from. We begin at this stage to understand the true significance of the dictum: Thy Will Be Done!

When we arrive at this stage, we are ready to merge our self in the True Self. We are ready for self-surrender — the next crucial step on the path.

The Guru is the ocean of grace; he is also the transmitter of grace — but we have to yearn for this grace, we have to allow the Guru to work on us, so that we may receive his grace.

Chapter 31
Start NOW!

Start NOW!

A man went to a homoeopath doctor complaining of pain in the knee. The doctor gave him some pills. After a week, the man met the doctor in a shop. The doctor inquired about his pain. The man responded that there was no improvement whatsoever. The doctor asked if he had taken the medicine. The man said, "O those pills. They are still in my pocket."

Friends, pills in the pocket will not help. So also, merely reading this book will not help much.

If you want to achieve your goals, whether they are material or spiritual, you need to act. If you want to change your life, you need to put the teachings into practice. Pick up one or two simple ideals that appeal to you, and make them a part of your life. A holy man once said, "If you have spent your whole life in gaining one good quality and giving up one bad one, you have not lived in vain."

A youngster, who came to meet me, told me very politely that apart from his work at the office, he hardly had enough time to devote to his essential activities in a 14-hour working day; there was no question of spending time on anything else.

"May I know what are your essential activities, as you call them?" I asked him politely.

"Well, I check my email and send replies, and that take

30 minutes," he began. "Then, I have to catch up with my friends on facebook and that takes at least an hour. I watch TV for about 2 hours and it's the only relaxation I have at home!"

"So you spend 23 days in the year just processing your email; you spend 46 days of the year just catching up with your friends on facebook and you spend 91 days of the year watching TV... that makes about 160 days of the year, right?"

"Wait a minute! I said no such thing! I said that I spent half an hour everyday on email and..."

"Yes, I know," I replied, smiling. "All I've done is add up the minutes to show you how much time you are investing in your 'essential' activities. Time is money, they say, don't they?"

The young man was taken aback to realise that he was spending nearly 23 weeks or the better part of six months in these 'essential' activities! And he claimed that he did not have five minutes to go over his meaningful actions during the day!

I am afraid this is the case with many of us. The email and facebook might be replaced by telephone, chatting, browsing or 'gaming' as they call it now; but we all spend the equivalent of several weeks every year in such activities, and we imagine that we are so busy that we do not have time for such pursuits as prayer, reflection, introspection, etc. As for meditation or other disciplines, well, that is meant for senior citizens, is it not?

We receive countless reminders every day, telling us

that we are here on earth, but as pilgrims. Sooner or later, the call will come, when we will have to bid adieu to all that we hold dear and cross over to the Other Shore. We need to ask our self the question, "What will we carry with us? Are we gathering the treasure imperishable, or are we frittering away our precious lives in vain pursuits?"

Time is fleeting! If we are to make the most of this life, the time to begin is NOW!

There are some days when you don't feel like doing whatever it is you're supposed to do that day to move towards your goal. Well, instead of thinking about how hard it is, and how long it will take, tell yourself that you just have to start. Once you start, it is never as hard as you thought it would be.

Try it now:

- Identify the most important thing you have to do today to achieve your goal.
- Decide to do just the first little part of it — just the first minute or two. Getting started is the only thing that matters now.
- Clear away distractions. Turn everything off. Close all programs. There should just be you, and your task towards achieving your goal.
- Sit there, and focus on getting started. Not doing the whole task, just starting.
- Pay attention to your mind, as it starts to have urges to switch to another task. You will have urges

check email or facebook or twitter or your favourite website. You will want to play a game or make a call or do something else. Notice these urges.

- But don't move. Notice the urges, but sit still, and let them pass. Urges build up in intensity, then pass, like a wave. Let each one pass.

- Notice also your mind trying to justify not doing the task. Also let these self-rationalising thoughts pass.

- Now just take one small action to get started. As tiny a step as possible. Get started and the rest will flow.